STILL STEAMING

A Guide to Britain's Standard Gauge Steam Railways 2013-2014

EDITOR
John Robinson

Seventeenth Edition

RAILWAY LOCATOR MAP

The numbers shown on this map relate to the page numbers for each railway. Pages 5-6 contain an alphabetical listing of the railways featured in this guide. Please note that the markers on this map show the approximate location only.

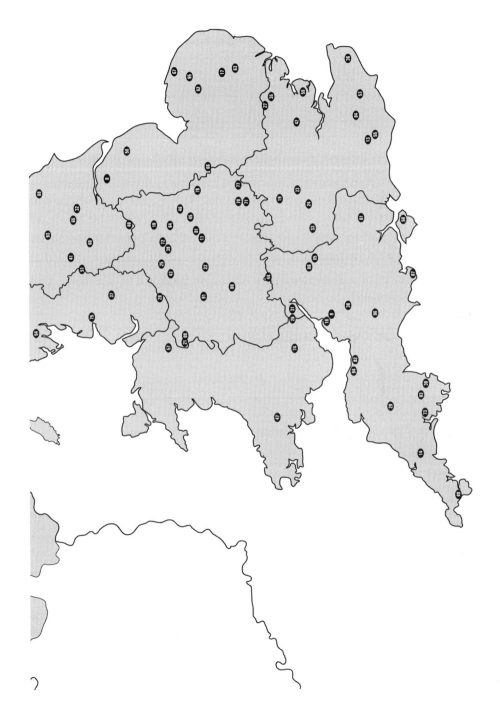

FOREWORD & ACKNOWLEDGEMENTS

We were greatly impressed by the friendly and cooperative manner of the staff and helpers of the railways which we selected to appear in this book, and wish to thank them for the help they have given. In addition we wish to thank Bob Budd (cover design) and Michael Robinson (page layouts) for their help and also Jonathan James who has provided us with photographs for several railways.

Although we believe that the information contained in this guide is accurate at the time of going to press, we, and the Railways and Museums itemised, are unable to accept liability for any loss, damage, distress or injury suffered as a result of any inaccuracies. Furthermore, we and the Railways are unable to guarantee operating and opening times which may always be subject to cancellation without notice.

We realise that other UK Standard Gauge railways are operating or about to resume operating (notably, the Eden Valley Railway), and we hope to include this in a future edition of Still Steaming.

At the time of going to press there was some doubt as to whether passenger trains would operate during 2013 at The Dartmoor Railway and the Weardale Railway after the American owners of both suspended services. It is hoped that passenger services will be scheduled later in 2013 on each of these railways and we suggest readers contact them directly for further information.

If you feel we should include other locations or information in future editions, please let us know so that we may give them consideration. We would like to thank you for buying this guide and wish you 'Happy Steaming'!

John Robinson
EDITOR

Note: Further copies of our railway guides, Still Steaming, Little Puffers and Tiny Trains may be obtained, post free, from our address below or ordered on-line via our web site –

www.stillsteaming.com

British Library Cataloguing in Publication Data
A catalogue record for this book is available from the British Library

ISBN-13: 978-1-86223-264-8

Copyright © 2013, MARKSMAN PUBLICATIONS. (01472 696226)
72 St. Peter's Avenue, Cleethorpes, N.E. Lincolnshire, DN35 8HU, England

Manufactured in the UK by Ashford Colour Press Ltd.

COVER PICTURE

Taken by John Faulkner on 5th November 2012, the photo shows the 1891-built O2 Class locomotive No. 24 'Calbourne', hauling former London, Brighton & South Coast Railway composite bogie coach No. S6349 (built 1924) and former South-Eastern & Chatham Railway bogie 4-compartment brake third Np. 4145 (built 1911), as the train passes through the outskirts of Briddlesford Copse on the approach to Wootton Station on the Isle of Wight Steam Railway.

CONTENTS

Locator Map (North) 2
Locator Map (South) 3
Foreword & Acknowledgments 4
Contents 5-6
Alderney Railway 7
Appleby Frodingham Railway Preservation Society 8
Avon Valley Railway 9
Barrow Hill Roundhouse Railway Centre 10
The Battlefield Line 11
Beamish – The Living Museum of the North 12
The Bluebell Railway 13
Bodmin & Wenford Railway 14
Bo'ness & Kinneil Railway 15
Bowes Railway 16
Bressingham Steam Museum 17
Bristol Harbour Railway 18
Buckinghamshire Railway Centre 19
Caledonian Railway 20
Cambrian Heritage Railways 21
Chasewater Railway 22
Chinnor & Princes Risborough Railway 23
Cholsey & Wallingford Railway 24
Churnet Valley Railway 25
Coleford GWR Museum 26
Colne Valley Railway 27
Crewe Heritage Centre 28
The Dartmoor Railway 29
Dartmouth Steam Railway 30
Dean Forest Railway 31
Derwent Valley Light Railway 32
Didcot Railway Centre 33
Downpatrick & County Down Railway 34
East Anglian Railway Museum 35
East Kent Light Railway 36
East Lancashire Railway 37
East Somerset Railway 38
Ecclesbourne Valley Railway 39
Elsecar Heritage Railway 40
Embsay & Bolton Abbey Steam Railway 41
Epping Ongar Railway 42
Foxfield Steam Railway 43

Gloucestershire Warwickshire Railway 44
Great Central Railway 45
Great Central Railway – Nottingham 46
Gwili Railway 47
Head of Steam – Darlington Railway Museum 48
Helston Railway 49
Isle of Wight Steam Railway 50
Keighley & Worth Valley Railway 51
The Keith & Dufftown Railway 52
Kent & East Sussex Railway 53
Lakeside & Haverthwaite Railway 54
The Lavender Line 55
Lincolnshire Wolds Railway 56
Llangollen Railway 57
Locomotion – The National Railway Museum at Shildon 58
Mangapps Railway Museum 59
The Middleton Railway 60
Mid-Hants Railway (The Watercress Line) 61
Mid-Norfolk Railway 62
Mid-Suffolk Light Railway Museum 63
Midland Railway – Butterley 64
National Railway Museum – York 65
Nene Valley Railway 66
North Norfolk Railway 67
North Tyneside Steam Railway 68
North Yorkshire Moors Railway 69
Northampton & Lamport Railway 70
Northamptonshire Ironstone Railway Trust 71
Peak Rail PLC 72
Plym Valley Railway 73
Pontypool & Blaenavon Railway 74
Ribble Steam Railway 75
Royal Deeside Railway 76
Rushden Transport Museum 77
Rutland Railway Museum 78
Scottish Industrial Railway Centre 79
Severn Valley Railway 80
Snibston Colliery Railway 81
Somerset & Dorset Railway Trust Museum 82
South Devon Railway 83
Spa Valley Railway 84
Steam – Museum of the Great Western Railway 85
Strathspey Steam Railway 86
Swanage Railway 87
Swindon & Cricklade Railway 88
Tanat Valley Light Railway 89
Tanfield Railway 90
Telford Steam Railway 91
Weardale Railway 92
Wensleydale Railway 93
West Somerset Railway 94
Whitwell & Reepham Railway 95
Yeovil Railway Centre 96

ALDERNEY RAILWAY

Address: P.O. Box 1075, Alderney, Channel Islands GY9 3DA	**Nº of Steam Locos**: None at present
Telephone Nº: None	**Nº of Other Locos**: 2
Year Formed: 1978	**Nº of Members**: 50
Location of Line: Braye Harbour to Mannez Quarry, Alderney	**Annual Membership Fee**: £15.00
	Approx Nº of Visitors P.A.: 2,000+
Length of Line: 2 miles	**Gauge**: Standard
	Web site: www.alderneyrailway.com

Photo courtesy of David Staines

GENERAL INFORMATION

Nearest Mainline Station: Not applicable
Nearest Bus Station: Not applicable
Car Parking: Available on site
Coach Parking: Available on site
Souvenir Shop(s): Yes
Food & Drinks: None at the Railway itself but available nearby

SPECIAL INFORMATION

The original line was built during the 1840s to assist in the construction of the large breakwater in Braye Harbour and fortifications on the island.
The line itself opened in 1847 and was the first nationalised railway run by the Admiralty.

OPERATING INFORMATION

Opening Times: Every Sunday and most Bank Holidays from Easter until the end of September and also on Saturdays in July and August. A Santa Special operates in December. Please contact the railway for further information. Trains usually run at 2.30pm and 3.30pm.
Steam Working: None at present
Prices: Adult Return £4.50
　　　　　Child Return £3.00

Detailed Directions:
The Railway is situated adjacent to Braye Harbour.

APPLEBY FRODINGHAM R.P.S.

Address: Appleby Frodingham Railway Preservation Society, P.O. Box 1, Scunthorpe   DN16 1BP
Telephone Nº: (01652) 656661
Year Formed: 1990
Location of Line: Tata Steelworks, Scunthorpe

Length of Line: 15 miles used on tours from almost 100 miles of track
Nº of Steam Locos: 2
Nº of Other Locos: 3
Nº of Members: 60
Gauge: Standard
Web site: www.afrps.co.uk

GENERAL INFORMATION

Nearest Mainline Station: Scunthorpe (1 mile)
Nearest Bus Station: Scunthorpe (½ mile)
Car Parking: Large free car park at the site
Coach Parking: At the site
Souvenir Shop(s): Yes – at the Loco Shed
Food & Drinks: Available at the Loco Shed

SPECIAL INFORMATION

The Society operates 15 mile Rail and Brake Van tours of the Tata steelworks site (which covers almost 12 square miles) using its extensive internal railway system.

OPERATING INFORMATION

Opening Times: Selected weekends throughout the year which <u>must</u> be pre-booked via (01652) 657053 or e-mail – bookings@afrps.co.uk
Private Hire of a train is now available for parties and anniversaries with use of the Lounge coach.
Steam Working: Most active days. Ask for further details when booking.
Prices: Free – but the society relies on donations which are collected at the end of each tour.
Please note that children cannot be carried on Brake Van tours due to the open verandahs.

Detailed Directions by Car:
Exit the M180 at Junction 4 and take the A18 into Scunthorpe. Turn right at the roundabout by Morrisons supermarket and follow the road along for approximately ½ mile. Turn right into Entrance E. Car parking is available on the left and the path to the station is on the right.   SatNav users please enter: DN16 1XA

AVON VALLEY RAILWAY

Address: Bitton Station, Bath Road, Bitton, Bristol BS30 6HD **Telephone N°**: (0117) 932-5538 **Year Formed**: 1973 **Location of Line**: Midway between Bristol and Bath on A431 **Length of Line**: 3 miles	**N° of Steam Locos**: 6 **N° of Other Locos**: 5 **N° of Members**: Approximately 700 **Annual Membership Fee**: £15.00 **Approx N° of Visitors P.A.**: 80,000 **Gauge**: Standard **Web site**: www.avonvalleyrailway.org **E-mail**: info@avonvalleyrailway.org

GENERAL INFORMATION

Nearest Mainline Station: Keynsham (1½ miles)
Nearest Bus Station: Bristol or Bath (7 miles)
Car Parking: Available at Bitton Station
Coach Parking: Available at Bitton Station
Souvenir Shop(s): Yes
Food & Drinks: Yes

SPECIAL INFORMATION

The line has been extended through the scenic Avon Valley towards Bath and a new platform is now open linking with walks along the River Avon and local Public Houses.

OPERATING INFORMATION

Opening Times: Every Sunday and some Saturdays from Easter to October and on weekends during December. Also Bank Holiday Mondays, Wednesdays in June and July and Tuesdays to Thursdays during School Holidays. Also open for Santa Specials over Christmas.
Open 10.30am to 5.00pm.
Steam Working: 11.00am to 4.00pm
Prices: Adult £6.50   (£7.00 on Steam Days)
　　　　　Child £5.00   (£5.50 on Steam Days)
　　　　　Family Tickets £18.00   (£19.50 Steam Days)
　　　　　Senior Citizens £5.50   (£6.00 Steam Days)

Detailed Directions by Car:
From All Parts: Exit the M4 at Junction 18. Follow the A46 towards Bath and at the junction with the A420 turn right towards Bristol. At Bridge Yate turn left onto the A4175 and continue until you reach the A431. Turn right and Bitton Station is 100 yards on the right.

BARROW HILL ROUNDHOUSE RAILWAY CENTRE

Address: Barrow Hill Roundhouse, Campbell Drive, Barrow Hill, Staveley, Chesterfield S43 2PR	**Nº of Steam Locos**: 12
	Nº of Other Locos: Over 40
	Nº of Members: Approximately 400
Telephone Nº: (01246) 472450	**Annual Membership Fee**: £19.00 (Adult)
Year Formed: 1998	**Approx Nº of Visitors P.A.**: 30,000
Location: Staveley, near Chesterfield	**Gauge**: Standard
Length of Line: ¾ mile	**Web site**: www.barrowhill.org

GENERAL INFORMATION

Nearest Mainline Station: Chesterfield (3½ miles)
Nearest Bus Station: Chesterfield (3 miles)
Car Parking: Space available for 300 cars
Coach Parking: Available
Souvenir Shop(s): Yes
Food & Drinks: Yes – buffet

SPECIAL INFORMATION

Britain's last remaining operational railway roundhouse provides storage and repair facilities for standard gauge steam, diesel and electric locomotives.

OPERATING INFORMATION

Opening Times: Open at weekends throughout the year (except for the Christmas and New Year period), from 10.00am to 4.00pm.
Steam Working: Special open days only. 2013 dates: Rail Ale Festival on 17th & 18th May; Roundhouse Open Day on 29th & 30th June; 'Barrow Hill Live Celebrating Doncaster 160' on 28th & 29th September. Please phone for further information or check the railway's web site.
Prices: Entry is by donation only but charges apply for Special Event days.

Detailed Directions by Car:
Exit the M1 at Junction 30 and take the A619 to Staveley (about 3½ miles). Pass through Staveley, turn right at Troughbrook Road. Continue along for ½ mile, pass under the railway bridge and take the turn immediately on the right. Turn left onto Campbell Drive and the Roundhouse is on the left. The railway is signposted with Brown Tourist signs.

THE BATTLEFIELD LINE

Address: The Battlefield Line, Shackerstone Station, Shackerstone, Warwickshire   CV13 6NW
Telephone N°: (01827) 880754
Year Formed: 1968
Location of Line: North West of Market Bosworth
Length of Line: 5 miles

N° of Steam Locos: 5
N° of Other Locos: 20
N° of Members: 500 approximately
Annual Membership Fee: £15.00 Adult; £35.00 Family
Approx N° of Visitors P.A.: 60,000
Gauge: Standard
Web site: www.battlefieldline.co.uk

GENERAL INFORMATION

Nearest Mainline Station: Nuneaton or Hinckley (both 12 miles)
Nearest Bus Station: Nuneaton & Hinckley (12 miles)
Car Parking: Ample free parking available
Coach Parking: At Market Bosworth Station
Souvenir Shop(s): At Shackerstone Station
Food & Drinks: Yes – Buffets available at all stations

SPECIAL INFORMATION

Travel from the Grade II listed Shackerstone Station through the beautiful Leicestershire countryside with views of the adjoining Ashby Canal. Arrive at the award-winning Shenton Station and explore Bosworth Battlefield (1485) before making the return journey.

OPERATING INFORMATION

Operating Info: 2013 dates: Weekends and Bank Holidays from 2nd March to 24th November and Santa Specials on weekends from 30th November to Christmas Eve. Also open on Wednesday afternoons in July and August. Please check the web site for further details.
Opening Times: 10.00am to 6.00pm
Steam Working: From 11.15am to 4.00pm during high season and Sundays.
Prices: Adult Return £10.00
Child Return £5.50 (ages 5-15 years)
O.A.P. Return £8.00
Family Ticket £27.00
(2 adults and 3 children)

Detailed Directions by Car:
Follow the brown tourist signs from the A444 or A447 heading towards the market town of Market Bosworth. Continue towards the villages of Congerstone & Shackerstone and finally to Shackerstone Station. Access is only available via the Old Trackbed.

BEAMISH –
THE LIVING MUSEUM OF THE NORTH

Address: Beamish – The Living Museum of the North, Co. Durham DH9 0RG **Telephone Nº**: (0191) 370-4000 **Year Formed**: 1970 **Length of Line**: ½ mile	**Nº of Steam Locos**: 11 **Nº of Other Locos**: 2 **N.B.**: Not all Locos are on display **Approx Nº of Visitors P.A.**: 500,000 **Web site**: www.beamish.org.uk

GENERAL INFORMATION

Nearest Mainline Station: Newcastle Central (8 miles); Durham City (12 miles)
Nearest Bus Station: Newcastle (8 miles); Durham (12 miles)
Car Parking: Free parking for 2,000 cars
Coach Parking: Free parking for 40 coaches
Souvenir Shop(s): Yes
Food & Drinks: Yes – self service tea room, licensed period Public House, Coffee shop and a coal-fired Fish & Chip shop!

SPECIAL INFORMATION

A replica of William Hedley's famous 1813 locomotive "Puffing Billy" steams on the Pockerley Waggonway at Beamish alongside replicas of Locomotion and the Steam Elephant.

OPERATING INFORMATION

Opening Times: Open all year round: from 10.00am to 4.00pm in the Winter (November to March). Closed on Mondays and Fridays in the Winter. Open from 10.00am to 5.00pm during the Summer (April to October). Check for Christmas opening times.
N.B. Mid-week winter visits are centred on the Town, Pit Village and Tramway only. Other areas are closed and admission prices are reduced.
Allow 4-5 hours for a Summer visit and two hours in the Winter.
Steam Working: Daily during the Summer
Prices: Adult £17.50 in Summer
　　　　　Child £10.00 in Summer
　　　　　Senior Citizen £13.00 in Summer
Children under 5 are admitted free.
Special Family Tickets are available.
Tickets allow unlimited free return visits for 12 months from the date of first visit.

Detailed Directions by Car:
From North & South: Follow the A1(M) to Junction 63 (Chester-le-street) and then take A693 for 4 miles towards Stanley; From North-West: Take the A68 south to Castleside near Consett and follow the signs on the A692 and A693 via Stanley.

THE BLUEBELL RAILWAY

Address: The Bluebell Railway, Sheffield Park Station, near Uckfield TN22 3QL
Telephone Nº: (01825) 720800
Year Formed: 1959
Location: Near Uckfield, East Sussex
Length of Line: 11 miles
Web site: www.bluebell-railway.com

Nº of Steam Locos: Over 30 with up to 3 in operation on any given day
Nº of Other Locos: –
Nº of Members: 10,000
Annual Membership Fee: £20.00 Adult
Approx Nº of Visitors P.A.: 175,000
Gauge: Standard

GENERAL INFORMATION

Nearest Mainline Station: East Grinstead (2 minute walk)
Nearest Bus Station: East Grinstead
Car Parking: Parking is available at Sheffield Park and Horsted Keynes Stations.
Coach Parking: Sheffield Park is best for coaches
Souvenir Shop(s): Yes
Food & Drinks: Yes – buffets and licensed bars & restaurant

SPECIAL INFORMATION

The Railway runs 'Golden Arrow' dining trains on Saturday evenings and Sunday lunchtimes. There is also a museum at Sheffield Park Station.

OPERATING INFORMATION

Opening Times: 2013 dates: Open every weekend throughout the year and also daily from 31st March to 27th October inclusive. Also open during School holidays and for Santa Specials during December. Open from approximately 10.30am to 5.30pm
Steam Working: As above
Prices: Adult Return £16.00
Child Return £8.00
Family Return £44.00 (2 adult + 3 child)

Detailed Directions by Car:
Sheffield Park Station is situated on the A275 Wych Cross to Lewes road. Horsted Keynes Station is signposted from the B2028 Lingfield to Haywards Heath road.

BODMIN & WENFORD RAILWAY

Address: Bodmin General Station, Losthwithiel Road, Bodmin, Cornwall PL31 1AQ
Telephone Nº: (0845) 1259678
Year Formed: 1984
Location of Line: Bodmin Parkway to Boscarne Junction, via Bodmin General
Length of Line: 6½ miles

Nº of Steam Locos: 11
Nº of Other Locos: 9
Nº of Members: 1,200
Annual Membership Fee: £14.00
Approx Nº of Visitors P.A.: 55,000
Gauge: Standard
Web site: www.bodminrailway.co.uk

GENERAL INFORMATION

Nearest Mainline Station: Bodmin Parkway (cross platform interchange with the Bodmin & Wenford Railway)
Car Parking: Free parking at Bodmin General
Coach Parking: Free parking at Bodmin General
Souvenir Shop(s): Yes
Food & Drinks: Yes

SPECIAL INFORMATION

The Railway has steep gradients and through tickets to "Bodmin & Wenford Railway" are available from all Mainline stations.

OPERATING INFORMATION

Opening Times: 2013 dates: Daily from 18th May to 16th October. Also daily during Easter week and other selected dates from February to May, October and November. Santa Specials run on 2nd, 3rd, 7th, 8th, 14th, 15th, 21st, 22nd, 23rd, 24th, 28th, 29th, 30th & 31st December and on 1st January.
Open 10.00am – 5.00pm on most days.
Steam Working: Most trains are steam-hauled except for most Saturdays when Diesels are used. Daily steam throughout August.
Prices: Adult All Day Rover £12.00
Senior Citizen All Day Rover £11.00
Child All Day Rover £6.00 (Under-3s free)
Family Day Rover £33.00 (2 adult + 4 child)

Detailed Directions by Car:
From the A30/A38/A389 follow the signs to Bodmin Town Centre then follow the brown tourist signs showing the steam engine logo to the Steam Railway on the B3268 Lostwithiel Road.

BO'NESS & KINNEIL RAILWAY

Address: Bo'ness Station, Union Street, Bo'ness, West Lothian   EH51 9AQ
Telephone N°: (01506) 822298
Year Opened: 1981
Location of Line: Bo'ness to Manuel
Length of Line: 5 miles

N° of Steam Locos: 26
N° of Other Locos: 25
N° of Members: 1,500
Annual Membership Fee: £22.00
Approx N° of Visitors P.A.: 70,000
Gauge: Standard
Web site: www.bkrailway.co.uk

GENERAL INFORMATION

Nearest Mainline Station: Linlithgow (3 miles)
Nearest Bus Station: Bo'ness (¼ mile)
Car Parking: Free parking at Bo'ness Station
Coach Parking: Free parking at Bo'ness Station
Souvenir Shop(s): Yes
Food & Drinks: Yes

SPECIAL INFORMATION

In addition to the ten-mile journey, passengers should visit Scotland's largest railway museum at Bo'ness Station. The Railway and Museum are operated by volunteers from The Scottish Railway Preservation Society.

OPERATING INFORMATION

Opening Times: 2013 dates: Weekends from 23rd March to 27th October. Also open for mid-week running on selected dates in April and October and on most days in July and August. Please contact the railway for further information. The museum is open daily from 29th March to 27th October.
Steam Working: On standard service days, 10.45am, 12.15pm and 2.05pm. The 3.35pm service may be diesel-hauled at weekends.
Prices: Adult Return £9.00   Child Return £5.00
Family Return £23.00   Concession Return £8.00
Note: Group discounts are also available.
Special fares may apply on Special Event Days.
Season Tickets for the Museum are £5.00

Detailed Directions by Car:
From Edinburgh: Take the M9 and exit at Junction 3. Then take the A904 to Bo'ness; From Glasgow: Take the M80 to M876 and then M9 (South). Exit at Junction 5 and take A904 to Bo'ness; From the North: Take M9 (South), exit at Junction 5, then take A904 to Bo'ness; From Fife: Leave the A90 after the Forth Bridge, then take A904 to Bo'ness.

BOWES RAILWAY

Address: Bowes Railway, Springwell Village, Gateshead, Tyne & Wear NE9 7QJ **Telephone Nº**: (0191) 416-1847 **Year Formed**: 1976 **Location of Line**: Springwell Village **Length of Line**: 1¼ miles	**Nº of Steam Locos**: 2 **Nº of Other Locos**: 5 **Nº of Members**: Approximately 70 **Annual Membership Fee**: £15.00 **Approx Nº of Visitors P.A.**: 5,000 **Gauge**: Standard **Web site**: www.bowesrailway.co.uk

GENERAL INFORMATION

Nearest Mainline Station: Newcastle Central (3 miles)
Nearest Bus Station: Gateshead Interchange (2 miles)
Car Parking: Free parking at site
Coach Parking: Free parking at site
Souvenir Shop(s): Yes
Food & Drinks: Yes

SPECIAL INFORMATION

Designed by George Stephenson and opened in 1826, the Railway is a scheduled Ancient Monument which operates unique preserved standard gauge rope-hauled inclines and steam hauled passenger trains.

OPERATING INFORMATION

Opening Times: The Springwell site is open for static viewing (no charges) on weekdays and some Saturdays throughout the year – 10.00am to 3.00pm.
Steam Working: As the 2013/2014 timetable had not been agreed when this book went to press, we suggest that readers check the railway's web site or contact the railway directly for further information.
Prices: No charges for visiting but admission fees are charged for special events. Please contact the railway or check the web site for further details.

Detailed Directions by Car:
From A1 (Northbound): Follow the A194(M) to the Tyne Tunnel and turn left at the sign for Springwell.
From A1 (Southbound): Take the turn off left for the B1288 to Springwell and Wrekenton.

BRESSINGHAM STEAM EXPERIENCE

Address: Bressingham Steam Museum, Bressingham, Diss, Norfolk   IP22 2AB
Telephone Nº: (01379) 686900
Year Formed: Mid 1950's
Location of Line: Bressingham, Near Diss
Length of Line: 5 miles in total (3 lines)

Nº of Steam Locos: 6 Standard gauge plus many others
Approx Nº of Visitors P.A.: 80,000+
Gauge: Standard, 2 foot, 10¼ inches and 15 inches
Web site: www.bressingham.co.uk

GENERAL INFORMATION

Nearest Mainline Station: Diss (2½ miles)
Nearest Bus Station: Bressingham (1¼ miles)
Car Parking: Free parking for 400 cars available
Coach Parking: Free parking for 30 coaches
Souvenir Shop(s): Yes
Food & Drinks: Yes

SPECIAL INFORMATION

In addition to Steam locomotives, Bressingham has a large selection of steam traction engines, fixed steam engines and also the National Dad's Army Museum, two extensive gardens and a water garden centre.

OPERATING INFORMATION

Opening Times: 2013 dates: Daily from 28th March to 3rd November. Open from 10.30am to 5.00pm and until 5.30pm in June, July and August.
Steam Working: Almost every operating day except for most Mondays and Tuesdays in March, April, May, June, July, September and October. Please contact the Museum for further details.
Prices: Adult £10.50 (non-Steam) £12.95 (Steam)
           Child £6.75 (non-Steam) £8.95 (Steam)
           Family £27.50 (non-Steam) £35.00 (Steam)
           Seniors £9.50 (non-Steam) £11.50 (Steam)
Note: Reduced entry charges apply for visitors who do not take railway rides.

Detailed Directions by Car:
From All Parts: Take the A11 to Thetford and then follow the A1066 towards Diss for Bressingham. The Museum is signposted by the brown tourist signs.

BRISTOL HARBOUR RAILWAY

Address: Princes Wharf, City Docks, Bristol   BS1 4RN
Telephone Nº: (0117) 903-1570
Year Formed: 1978
Location of Line: South side of the Floating Harbour
Length of Line: 1½ miles

Nº of Steam Locos: 2
Nº of Other Locos: 1
Approx Nº of Visitors P.A.: –
Gauge: Standard
Web site: mshed.org

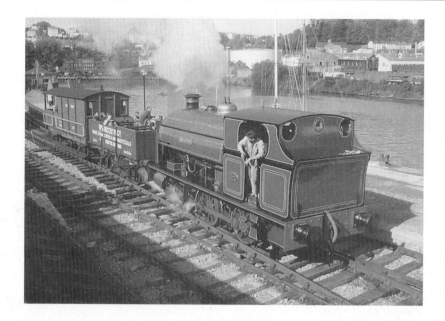

GENERAL INFORMATION

Nearest Mainline Station: Bristol Temple Meads (1 mile)
Nearest Bus Station: City Centre (½ mile)
Car Parking: Pay & Display adjacent to M Shed
Coach Parking: Pay & Display adjacent
Souvenir Shop(s): In the M Shed Museum
Food & Drinks: Café in the Museum

SPECIAL INFORMATION

The new M Shed museum opened in June 2011 and has since attracted over 1 million visitors. All the working exhibits have now resumed operation. Trains run alongside the harbour to link the M Shed with the SS Great Britain and Create Centre.

OPERATING INFORMATION

Opening Times: 2013 dates: 30th & 31st March; 1st, 13th, 14th, 27th and 28th April; 4th, 5th, 6th, 26th & 27th May; 13th, 14th, 15th, 16th, 29th & 30th June; 13th, 14th, 27th & 28th July; 24th, 25th & 26th August; 14th, 15th, 28th & 29th September; 12th, 13th, 26th & 27th October; 2nd & 3rd November. Trains run from 11.00am to 5.00pm.
Steam Working: Please contact the railway for further details.
Prices: All-day Rover £4.00
M Shed to Create Return £3.00
M Shed to Create Single £2.00
M Shed to SS Great Britain Return £2.00
M Shed to SS Great Britain Single £1.00
Note: Children under the age of 6 travel for free.

Detailed Directions by Car:
From All Parts: Follow signs to Bristol City Centre and then the Brown Tourist signs for the Museum. A good landmark to look out for are the 4 huge quayside cranes.

BUCKINGHAMSHIRE RAILWAY CENTRE

Address: Quainton Road Station, Quainton, Aylesbury, Bucks. HP22 4BY **Telephone Nº**: (01296) 655720 **Year Formed**: 1969 **Location of Line**: At Quainton on the old Metropolitan/Great Central Line **Length of Line**: 2 × ½ mile demo tracks	**Nº of Steam Locos**: 30 **Nº of Other Locos**: 6 **Nº of Members**: 1,000 **Annual Membership Fee**: £25.00 **Approx Nº of Visitors P.A.**: 35,000 **Gauge**: Standard (also a Miniature line) **Recorded Info. Line**: (01296) 655450

GENERAL INFORMATION

Nearest Mainline Station: Aylesbury (6 miles)
Nearest Bus Station: Aylesbury
Car Parking: Free parking for 500 cars available
Coach Parking: Free parking for 10 coaches
Souvenir Shop(s): Yes
Food & Drinks: Yes

SPECIAL INFORMATION

In addition to a large collection of locomotives and carriages, the Centre has an extensive ½ mile outdoor miniature railway system operated by the Vale of Aylesbury Model Engineering Society.

Web site: www.bucksrailcentre.org
E-mail: office@bucksrailcentre.org

OPERATING INFORMATION

Opening Times: Tuesday to Thursday for restricted viewing only from Easter to October. Open 10.30am to 4.30pm.
Steam Working: Sundays and Bank Holidays from April to October and also on Wednesdays during the School holidays.
Prices: Adult £5.50, £10.00 and £12.00
 Child £3.50, £7.00 and £9.00
 (Under 5's travel free of charge)
 Senior Citizen £4.50, £9.00 and £11.00
 Family £15.00, £27.00 and £33.00
 (2 adults + up to 4 children)
Note: Prices shown above are for restricted viewing, Steam Days and Special Event days respectively.

Detailed Directions by Car:
The Buckinghamshire Railway Centre is signposted off the A41 Aylesbury to Bicester Road at Waddesdon and off the A413 Buckingham to Aylesbury road at Whitchurch. Junctions 7, 8 and 9 of the M40 are all close by.

CALEDONIAN RAILWAY

Address: The Station, 2 Park Road, Brechin, Angus DD9 7AF	**N° of Steam Locos**: 5
Telephone N°: (01561) 377760	**N° of Other Locos**: 10
Year Formed: 1979	**N° of Members**: 250
Location of Line: From Brechin to the Bridge of Dun	**Annual Membership Fee**: Adult £12.00; Family £15.00; OAP/Junior £5.00
Length of Line: 4 miles	**Approx N° of Visitors P.A.**: 12,000
	Gauge: Standard
	Web site: www.caledonianrailway.com

GENERAL INFORMATION

Nearest Mainline Station: Montrose (4½ miles)
Nearest Bus Station: Brechin (200 yards)
Car Parking: Ample free parking at both Stations
Coach Parking: Free parking at both Stations
Souvenir Shop(s): Yes
Food & Drinks: Light refreshments are available

SPECIAL INFORMATION

Brechin Station is the only original Terminus station in preservation.

OPERATING INFORMATION

Opening Times: 2013 dates: Easter specials on 31st March; Christmas specials in December and every weekend from 25th May to 1st September. Also open for some other Special Events throughout the year. Please contact the Railway for further details. Trains usually run from 10.30am to 5.05pm.
Steam Working: Steam service on every Sunday.
Prices: Adult Return   £7.00
            Child Return   £5.00   (Under-3s £1.00)
            Senior Citizen Return   £6.00
Higher fares may apply for Special Event days.

Detailed Directions by Car:

From South: For Brechin Station, leave the A90 at the Brechin turn-off and go straight through the Town Centre. Pass the Northern Hotel, take the 2nd exit at the mini-roundabout then it is 150 yards to Park Road/St. Ninian Square; From North: For Brechin Station, leave the A90 at the Brechin turn-off and go straight through Trinity Village. Turn left at the mini-roundabout, it is then 250 yards to Park Road/St. Ninian Square. Bridge of Dun is situated half way between Brechin and Montrose. (Follow tourist signs).

CAMBRIAN HERITAGE RAILWAYS

Address: Old Station Building, Oswald Street, Oswestry SY11 4RE **Telephone Nº:** (01691) 688763 **Year Formed:** 2009 **Location of Line:** Llynclys and Oswestry **Length of Line:** Almost 1 mile at each site	**Nº of Steam Locos:** 3 (under repair) **Nº of Other Locos:** 2 DMUs + others **Nº of Members:** 500+ **Annual Membership Fee:** £15.00 **Approx Nº of Visitors P.A.:** 5,000 **Gauge:** Standard **Web site:** www.cambrianrailways.com

GENERAL INFORMATION

Nearest Mainline Station: Gobowen (3 miles from Oswestry – 7 miles from Llynclys)
Nearest Bus Station: Oswestry
Car Parking: Limited parking at both sites
Coach Parking: Limited parking. Please contact the railway for further information.
Souvenir Shop(s): Yes
Food & Drinks: Available

SPECIAL INFORMATION

Cambrian Heritage Railways Ltd. lease 8½ miles of the former Cambrian Railways from Shropshire Council. The former Cambrian Railways Society and Trust are incorporated into CHR. The track is still in place from Gobowen to Llan y Blodwel. There are operations at Oswestry and Llynclys and a museum on site at Oswestry.

OPERATING INFORMATION

Opening Times: 2013 dates: Open every Saturday, Sunday and Bank Holiday from Easter to the 29th September. Also open on Sundays in October and December. The Oswestry site only operates on Saturdays during the school holidays.
Trains run from 11.00am to 4.00pm.
Steam Working: Please contact the Railway for information.
Prices: Adults £3.00
Concessions £1.50
Family £8.00 (2 adults + 2 children)
Note: All the above prices are for "Full Day Rover" tickets on Diesel-hauled days. Higher fares may apply on Steam-hauled days.

Detailed Directions by Car:
The Llynclys site is situated on the B4396 approximately 5 miles southwest of Oswestry, just off the A483 heading towards Welshpool. Turn left at Llyncly Crossroads towards Knockin. The entrance to the site is on the right after about 400 yards, immediately over the railway bridge. The Oswestry site is near the town centre and is clearly signposted.

CHASEWATER RAILWAY (THE COLLIERY LINE)

Address: Chasewater Country Park,
Pool Lane, Burntwood, Staffs,
WS8 7NL
Telephone Nº: (01543) 452623
Year Re-formed: 1985
Location: Chasewater Country Park,
near Brownhills, Walsall
Length of Line: 2 miles

Nº of Steam Locos: 12
Nº of Other Locos: 15
Nº of Members: 500+
Annual Membership Fee: Adult £17.50;
Family £30.00; Concessions £12.50
Approx Nº of Visitors P.A.: 45,000
Gauge: Standard
Web site: www.chasewaterrailway.co.uk

GENERAL INFORMATION

Nearest Mainline Station: Walsall or Cannock
(both approximately 8 miles)
Nearest Bus Station: Lichfield (8½ miles)
Car Parking: Free parking in Chasewater Park
Coach Parking: Free parking in Chasewater Park
Souvenir Shop(s): Yes
Food & Drinks: Yes

SPECIAL INFORMATION

Chasewater Railway is based on the Cannock Chase
& Wolverhampton Railway opened in 1856. The
railway passed into the hands of the National Coal
Board which then ceased using the line in 1965.
Trains operate between Brownhills West and
Chasetown.

OPERATING INFORMATION

Opening Times: 2013 dates: Sundays and Bank
Holiday Mondays throughout the year plus
Saturdays from Easter to 26th October and selected
mid-week operating days. Please contact the railway
for further details. Also Santa Specials in December.
A regular service runs from 11.00am on operating
days.
Steam Working: Please check the web site or phone
for further details.
Prices: Adult Return £3.95
Child Return £2.95 (Under-5s ride free)
Family Return £9.95
All tickets offer unlimited rides on the day of issue.

Detailed Directions by Car:
Chasewater Country Park is situated in Brownhills off the A5 southbound near the junction of the A5 with the
A452 Chester Road. Follow the Brown tourist signs on the A5 for the Country Park.

CHINNOR & PRINCES RISBOROUGH RAILWAY

Address: Station Road, Chinnor, Oxon, OX39 4ER
Telephone Nº: (01844) 353535 (timetable)
Year Formed: 1989
Location: The Icknield Line, Chinnor
Length of Line: 3½ miles
Gauge: Standard

Nº of Steam Locos: 1
Nº of Other Locos: 6
Nº of Members: 1,000
Annual Membership Fee: Adult £15.00; Family £25.00; Child £5.00; OAP £10.00
Approx Nº of Visitors P.A.: 15,000
Web Site: www.chinnorrailway.co.uk

GENERAL INFORMATION

Nearest Mainline Station: Princes Risborough (4 miles)
Nearest Bus Station: High Wycombe (10 miles)
Car Parking: Free parking at site
Coach Parking: Prior arrangement preferred but not necessary
Souvenir Shop(s): Yes
Food & Drinks: Soft drinks and light snacks in Station Buffet. Buffet usually available on trains.

SPECIAL INFORMATION

The Chinnor & Princes Risborough Railway operates the remaining 3½ mile section of the former GWR Watlington Branch from Chinnor to Thame Junction.

OPERATING INFORMATION

Opening Times: 2013 dates: Sundays and Bank Holiday Mondays from 10th March to 27th October and also Santa Specials on weekends in December plus Mince Pie Specials from 29th to 31st December. Please check the railway's website for details of other bookable special and evening events during the year.
Steam Working: Operates from 11.00am to 4.30pm on Sundays and Bank Holidays
Prices: Adult Return £10.00   Child Return £5.00
Family Return £25.00 (2 adult + 2 child)
Senior Citizen Return £9.00

Detailed Directions by Car:
From All Parts: The railway at Chinnor is situated in Station Road just off the B4009. Junction 6 of the M40 is 4 miles away and Princes Risborough 4 miles further along the B4009. Once in Chinnor follow the brown Tourist signs to the railway.

CHOLSEY & WALLINGFORD RAILWAY

Address: Wallingford Station, 5 Hithercroft Road, Wallingford, Oxon, OX10 9GQ **Telephone Nº**: (01491) 835067 (24hr info) **Year Formed**: 1981 **Location of Line**: Wallingford, Oxon. **Length of Line**: 2½ miles	**Nº of Steam Locos**: Visiting locos only **Nº of Other Locos**: 4 **Nº of Members**: 250 **Annual Membership Fee**: £12.50 **Approx Nº of Visitors P.A.**: 9,700 **Gauge**: Standard **Web**: www.cholsey-wallingford-railway.com

GENERAL INFORMATION

Nearest Mainline Station: Joint station at Cholsey
Nearest Bus Station: Wallingford (¼ mile)
Car Parking: Off road parking available
Coach Parking: Off road parking available
Souvenir Shop(s): Yes
Food & Drinks: Yes

SPECIAL INFORMATION

The Wallingford branch (now known as "The Bunk Line") was originally intended as a through line to Princes Risborough, via Watlington, but became the first standard gauge branch of Brunel's broad-gauge London to Bristol line.

OPERATING INFORMATION

Opening Times: Selected weekends from Easter until Christmas with trains running from 11.00am to 4.30pm – please phone the railway or check the web site for further details.
Steam Working: The railway will have visiting steam locomotives from time to time. Please contact the railway for further information.
Prices: Adult Return £8.00 (£6.00 diesel days)
  Child Return £4.50 (£3.50 diesel days)
  Concessionary Return £6.50 (£5.00 diesel)
  Family Return £23.00 (£17.00 diesel days)
  (2 adults + 2 children)
Prices: Prices may be subject to change for Engine visits and other special events.

Detailed Directions by Car:
From All Parts: Exit from the A34 at the Milton Interchange (between E. Ilsley and Abingdon). Follow signs to Didcot and Wallingford (A4130). Take Wallingford bypass, then turn left at the first roundabout (signposted Hithercroft Road). The Station is then ½ mile on the right.

CHURNET VALLEY RAILWAY

Address: Kingsley & Froghall Station, Froghall, Stoke-on-Trent   ST10 2HA
Telephone Nº: (01538) 750755
Year Formed: 1978
Location of Line: Kingsley & Froghall to Cheddleton
Length of Line: 5¼ miles (plus a further 8 miles when operating over Moorland &

City Railways, Cauldon Branch)
Nº of Steam Locos: 6 (2 in operation)
Nº of Other Locos: 11 (3 in operation)
Annual Membership Fee: £14.00
Approx Nº of Visitors P.A.: 70,000
Gauge: Standard
Web: www.churnet-valley-railway.co.uk

Photo courtesy of D.R. Gibson

GENERAL INFORMATION

Nearest Mainline Station: Stoke-on-Trent (12 miles)
Nearest Bus Station: Leek (5 miles)
Car Parking: Parking available on site
Coach Parking: Restricted space available at Kingsley & Froghall Station.
Souvenir Shop(s): Yes
Food & Drinks: Yes

SPECIAL INFORMATION

Cheddleton Station is a Grade II listed building, Consall is a sleepy halt with Victorian charm, whereas Kingsley & Froghall has been rebuilt in NSR style and includes disabled facilities and a tearoom.

OPERATING INFORMATION

Opening Times: 2013 dates: Sundays from Easter until the end of September; Saturdays during June, July and August; Every Wednesday in July and August and all Bank Holiday Mondays. Santa Specials run on weekends and Wednesdays in December (pre-booking required). Trains usually run from 10.30am on most operating days. Please contact the railway for further details.
Steam Working: Most operating days except for Diesel Gala days.
Prices: Adult Day Rover £11.00
Child Day Rover £5.00 (Ages 4 to 14)
Senior Citizen Day Rover £9.00
Family Ticket Day Rover £28.00

Detailed Directions by Car:
From All Parts: Take the M6 to Stoke-on-Trent and follow roads to Ashbourne or Leek. Cheddleton Station is off the A520 Leek to Stone road (SatNav ST13 7EE). Kingsley & Froghall Station is off the A52 Ashbourne Road.

Coleford GWR Museum

Address: The Old Railway Station, Railway Drive, Coleford GL16 8RH **Telephone N°**: (01594) 833569 **Year Formed**: 1988 **Location of Line**: Coleford **Length of Line**: 100 yards	**N° of Steam Locos**: 2 **N° of Other Locos**: – **Approx N° of Visitors P.A.**: Not known **Gauge**: 7¼ inches and Standard gauge **Web site**: www.colefordgwr.150m.com

GENERAL INFORMATION

Nearest Mainline Station: Lydney (7½ miles)
Nearest Bus Station: Gloucester (20 miles)
Car Parking: Low cost parking available on site
Coach Parking: Available
Souvenir Shop(s): Yes
Food & Drinks: Tea and Coffee available only

SPECIAL INFORMATION

Based in the 1883 Goods Shed at Coleford, the Museum chronicles the history of railways in the Forest of Dean.

OPERATING INFORMATION

Opening Times: 2013 dates: Saturday afternoons and Bank Holidays throughout the year and Fridays from Easter until 3rd November. Open from 2.30pm to 5.00pm and at other times by prior arrangement.
Steam Working: Easter Monday and other Bank Holidays. Please contact the Museum for details.
Prices: Adults £3.00 (admission to the museum)
          Children £2.00 (admission to the museum)
          Miniature Railway Rides £2.00
          Peckett Footplate Visit £2.00 (if steaming)

Detailed Directions by Car:
From All Parts: From the M50 take the A40 at Ross-on-Wye to Monmouth then the A4136 towards Cinderford. Turn off the A4136 into Coleford and the Museum is located in the Town Centre.

COLNE VALLEY RAILWAY

Address: Castle Hedingham Station, Yeldham Road, Castle Hedingham, Essex, CO9 3DZ
Telephone Nº: (01787) 461174
Year Formed: 1974
Location of Line: On A1017, 7 miles north-west of Braintree
Length of Line: Approximately 1 mile

Nº of Steam Locos: 4
Nº of Other Locos: 11
Nº of Members: 280
Annual Membership Fee: £11.00
Approx Nº of Visitors P.A.: 45,000
Gauge: Standard
Web Site: www.colnevalleyrailway.co.uk

GENERAL INFORMATION

Nearest Mainline Station: Braintree (7 miles)
Nearest Bus Station: Hedingham bus from Braintree stops at the Railway (except on Sundays)
Car Parking: Parking at the site
Coach Parking: Free parking at site
Souvenir Shop(s): Yes
Food & Drinks: Yes – on operational days. Also Pullman Sunday Lunches – bookings necessary.

SPECIAL INFORMATION

The railway has been re-built on a section of the old Colne Valley & Halstead Railway, with all buildings, bridges, signal boxes, etc. re-located on site.

OPERATING INFORMATION

Opening Times: 2013 dates: Trains run every Sunday and Bank Holiday weekend from 10th March to 27th October, Wednesdays and Thursdays in August and during the School Holidays. Pre-booked parties any time by arrangement and various other special events. Please check the web site for further details.
Steam Working: Sundays 10.30pm to 4.00pm, Bank Holidays from 10.30am to 4.00pm and 10.30am to 3.30pm on midweek operating days.
Prices: Adult – Steam days £9.00; Diesel £8.00
    Child – Steam £5.00; Diesel £4.00
    Family (2 adults + 3 children) –
        Steam £28.00; Diesel £22.00
    Senior Citizen – Steam £7.00; Diesel £6.00

Detailed Directions by Car:
The Railway is situated on the A1017 between Halstead and Haverhill, 7 miles north-west of Braintree.

CREWE HERITAGE CENTRE

Address: Vernon Way, Crewe, CW1 2DB	**Nº of Steam Locos:** 1
Telephone Nº: (01270) 212130	**Nº of Other Locos:** 2
Year Formed: 1987	**Approx Nº of Visitors P.A.:** 10,000
Location of Line: Crewe Heritage Centre	**Gauge:** 7¼ inches and Standard Gauge
Length of Line: 300 yards (Standard gauge) and 600 yards (7¼ inch gauge)	**Web site:** www.creweheritagecentre.co.uk

GENERAL INFORMATION

Nearest Mainline Station: Crewe (¾ mile)
Nearest Bus Station: Crewe (½ mile)
Car Parking: Available on site
Coach Parking: None
Souvenir Shop(s): Yes
Food & Drinks: Tea and Coffee only

SPECIAL INFORMATION

Crewe Heritage Centre is an operational base for numerous mainline steam charters with various locomotives present throughout the year.

OPERATING INFORMATION

Opening Times: Weekends and Bank Holidays from Easter until the end of September. Open 10.00am to 4.30pm.
Steam Working: Please contact the Centre for details.
Prices: Adults £6.00
Children £3.00
Concessions £3.00
Family Tickets £14.00

Detailed Directions by Car:
From All Parts: Exit the M6 at Junction 16 and take the A500 into Crewe. Follow the brown tourist signs for "The Railway Age". The Heritage Centre is adjacent to Crewe Railway Station and next to the Tesco Supermarket.

THE DARTMOOR RAILWAY

Address: Okehampton Station, Station Road, Okehampton   EX20 1EJ
Telephone Nº: (01837) 55164
Year Formed: 1997
Location of Line: Meldon Quarry to Coleford Junction

Length of Line: 15½ miles
Nº of Steam Locos: 1 + visiting locos
Nº of Other Locos: 2 and DMUs
Gauge: Standard
Web site: www.dartmoor-railway.co.uk

GENERAL INFORMATION

Nearest Mainline Station: Crediton
Nearest Bus Station: Okehampton
Car Parking: Okehampton Station and some spaces at Sampford Courtenay Station – all free of charge
Coach Parking: Okehampton Station
Souvenir Shop(s): Yes
Food & Drinks: Okehampton Buffet and Meldon Buffet are open on Bank Holidays and other operating days. The Buffets are fully licensed.

SPECIAL INFORMATION

The railway operates on the route of the old Southern Railway line through the mid-Devon countryside to the northern slopes of Dartmoor National Park.

OPERATING INFORMATION

Opening Times: 2013 dates: At the time of going to press, the American owners of the railway had suspended all passenger services pending further notice. It is hoped that some services will run later in 2013.
Please contact the railway for further information.
Steam Working: Please contact the railway for further information.
Prices: Vary depending upon the destination.
Please contact the railway for further information.

Detailed Directions by Car:
From All Parts: Take the A30 Exeter to Launceston dual carriageway and exit at the Okehampton turn-off. Once in town, follow the brown tourist signs up the hill to Okehampton Station.

Dartmouth Steam Railway & River Boat Company

Address: Queen's Park Station, Torbay Road, Paignton TQ4 6AF **Telephone N°**: (01803) 555872 **E-mail**: carolyn@dsrrb.co.uk **Year Formed**: 1973 **Location of Line**: Paignton to Kingswear **Length of Line**: 7 miles	**N° of Steam Locos**: 6 **N° of Other Locos**: 3 **N° of Members**: – **Annual Membership Fee**: – **Approx N° of Visitors P.A.**: 350,000 **Gauge**: Standard **Web site**: www.dartmouthrailriver.co.uk

GENERAL INFORMATION

Nearest Mainline Station: Paignton (adjacent)
Nearest Bus Station: Paignton (2 minutes walk)
Car Parking: Multi-storey or Mainline Station
Coach Parking: Multi-storey (3 minutes walk)
Souvenir Shop(s): Yes – at Paignton & Kingswear
Food & Drinks: Yes – at Paignton & Kingswear

SPECIAL INFORMATION

A passenger ferry is available from Kingswear Station across to Dartmouth. Combined excursions are also available including train and river trips.

OPERATING INFORMATION

Opening Times: Open daily from April to October (inclusive) and for Santa Specials during dates in December. Please contact the railway for further information.
Steam Working: Trains run throughout the day from 10.30am to 5.00pm.
Prices: Adult Return £13.50 (Includes ferry charge)
        Child Return £7.50 (Includes ferry charge)
        Concession Return £12.50 (Includes ferry)
        Family Return £35.50
    (2 adults and 2 children – Includes ferry charge)
Note: Cheaper fares are charged for shorter journeys

Detailed Directions by Car:
From All Parts: Take the M5 to Exeter and then the A380 to Paignton.

DEAN FOREST RAILWAY

Address: Norchard Centre, Forest Road; Lydney, Gloucestershire GL15 4ET	**Nº of Steam Locos:** 7 (4 working)
Telephone Nº: (01594) 845840	**Nº of Other Locos:** 18
Information Line: (01594) 843423 (24 hr.)	**Nº of Members:** 1,000
Year Formed: 1970	**Annual Membership Fee:** Adult £14.00; Family (4 persons) £17.00
Location of Line: Lydney, Gloucestershire	**Approx Nº of Visitors P.A.:** 35,000
Length of Line: 4½ miles	**Gauge:** Standard
	Web site: www.deanforestrailway.co.uk

GENERAL INFORMATION

Nearest Mainline Station: Lydney (200 metres)
Nearest Bus Station: Lydney Town (400 metres)
Car Parking: 600 spaces available at Norchard
Coach Parking: Ample space available
Souvenir Shop(s): Yes + a Museum
Food & Drinks: Yes – on operational days only

SPECIAL INFORMATION

Dean Forest Railway preserves the sole surviving line of the Severn and Wye Railway. The Railway has lengthened the line to a total of 4½ miles and Norchard to Parkend is now open for steam train operation giving a round trip of 9 miles.

OPERATING INFORMATION

Opening Times: 2013 dates: Norchard is open every day for viewing. Trains operate on Sundays from 17th February to 10th November, on most Wednesdays and Saturdays from 25th May to 12th October, Thursdays in August and various other dates. Phone or check the railway's web site for further details.

Steam Working: Most services are steam-hauled – check the web site or phone for details. Trains depart Norchard at various times from 10.35am to 3.30pm.

Prices: Adult Return £11.00 OAP Return £10.00
Child Return £5.00 (Under-5s free)
Family Ticket £30.00 (2 adults + 2 children)

Note: Fares may differ on Special Event days.

Detailed Directions by Car:
From M50 & Ross-on-Wye: Take the B4228 and B4234 via Coleford to reach Lydney. Norchard is located on the B4234, ¾ mile north of Lydney Town Centre; From Monmouth: Take the A4136 and B4431 onto the B4234 via Coleford; From South Wales: Take the M4 then M48 onto the A48 via Chepstow to Lydney; From Midlands/ Gloucester: Take the M5 to Gloucester then the A48 to Lydney; From the West Country: Take the M4 and M48 via the 'Old' Severn Bridge to Chepstow and then the A48 to Lydney.

DERWENT VALLEY LIGHT RAILWAY

Address: Murton Park, Murton Lane, Murton, York YO19 5UF	**N° of Steam Locos**: 1
Telephone N°: (01904) 489966	**N° of Other Locos**: 9
Year Formed: 1991	**N° of Members**: 80
Location of Line: Murton, near York	**Annual Membership Fee**: £15.00
Length of Line: ½ mile	**Approx N° of Visitors P.A.**: 15,000
Web site: www.dvlr.org.uk	**Gauge**: Standard
	E-mail: dvlr@hotmail.co.uk

GENERAL INFORMATION

Nearest Mainline Station: York (4 miles)
Nearest Bus Station: York (4 miles)
Car Parking: Large free car park at the site
Coach Parking: Free at the site
Souvenir Shop(s): Yes
Food & Drinks: Yes – as above

SPECIAL INFORMATION

The site is the remnants of the Derwent Valley Railway which was the last privately owned railway in England, originally opened in 1913.

OPERATING INFORMATION

Opening Times: 2013 dates: Sundays and Bank Holidays from 31st March until 29th September. Centenary Celebration Gala on 20th and 21st July. Santa Specials also run during dates in December.
Steam Working: Second and last Sunday in the month and Bank Holidays – 10.30am to 4.15pm.
Prices: Adult £6.00   Child £4.00
           Senior Citizens/Students £5.00
           Family Tickets £16.00 (2 adult + 4 children)
Note: Prices shown are for entry to the museum. Rides are free thereafter.

Detailed Directions by Car:
From All Parts: The railway is well signposted for the Yorkshire Museum of Farming from the A64 (York to Scarborough road), the A1079 (York to Hull road) and the A166 (York to Bridlington road).

DIDCOT RAILWAY CENTRE

Address: Didcot Railway Centre, Didcot, Oxfordshire OX11 7NJ **Telephone N°**: (01235) 817200 **Year Formed**: 1961 **Location of Line**: Didcot **Length of Line**: ¾ mile **Gauge**: Standard and 7 foot ¼ inch	**N° of Steam Locos**: 23 **N° of Other Locos**: 2 **N° of Members**: 4,400 **Annual Membership Fee**: Full £26.00; Over 60/Under 18 £18.00; Family £33.00 **Approx N° of Visitors P.A.**: 70,000 **Web Site**: www.didcotrailwaycentre.org.uk

GENERAL INFO

Nearest Mainline Station: Didcot Parkway (adjacent)
Nearest Bus Station: Buses to Didcot call at the Railway station
Car Parking: BR car park adjacent
Coach Parking: Further details on application
Souvenir Shop(s): Yes
Food & Drinks: Yes

SPECIAL INFO

The Centre is based on a Great Western Railway engine shed and is devoted to the re-creation of part of the GWR including Brunel's broad gauge railway and a newly built replica of the Fire Fly locomotive of 1840.

OPERATING INFO

Opening Times: 2013 dates: Weekends all year round, open daily during most school holidays and also from 25th May to 15th September. Weekends and Steam days open 10.30am to 5.00pm. Other days and during the Winter, open 10.30am to 3.30pm.
Steam Working: Bank Holidays and every weekend from 25th May until 1st September. Wednesdays from 24th July to 28th August. Please phone or check the web site for details of Autumn steam days.
Prices: Adult £5.00–£12.00
Child £4.00–£10.00
Senior Citizen £4.50–£8.50
Discounted family tickets are available (2 adults + 2 children) except for Thomas days and other special events. Prices vary depending on the events.

Detailed Directions by Car:
From East & West: Take the M4 to Junction 13 then the A34 and A4130 (follow brown Tourist signs to Didcot Railway Centre); From North: The Centre is signed from the A34 to A4130.

DOWNPATRICK & COUNTY DOWN RAILWAY

Address: Market Street, Downpatrick, Co. Down, Northern Ireland	**N⁰ of Steam Locos**: 3
Telephone N⁰: (07790) 802049	**N⁰ of Other Locos**: 5
Year Formed: 1985	**N⁰ of Members**: 200
Location of Line: Downpatrick	**Annual Membership Fee**: Adult £25.00,
Length of Line: 2 miles	Family £50.00, Concessions £20.00
Gauge: Irish Standard (5 foot 3 inches)	**Approx N⁰ of Visitors P.A.**: 13,000
	Web: www.downrail.co.uk

GENERAL INFORMATION

Nearest Mainline Station: –
Nearest Bus Station: Adjacent to Station
Car Parking: Ample parking adjacent to Station
Coach Parking: Ample parking adjacent to Station
Souvenir Shop(s): Yes
Food & Drinks: Yes

SPECIAL INFORMATION

This is the only operating Standard (5' 3") Gauge Heritage Railway in Ireland.

OPERATING INFORMATION

Opening Times: The Museum is open daily from June to September.
Steam Working: 2013 dates: Easter and May Bank Holiday weekends then weekends from 15th June to 15th September (includes August Bank Holiday). Also Halloween Ghost Trains on dates in October and Santa Specials on some dates in December. Please contact the railway for further details. Trains usually run from 2.00pm to 5.00pm.
Prices: Adult Return £5.50
             Child Return £4.50   (Under-3's ride free)
             Concessionary Return £4.50

Detailed Directions by Car:
From Belfast take the A7 Downpatrick Road. Upon arrival in Downpatrick, follow the brown tourist signs and the Railway Museum is adjacent to the bus station.

EAST ANGLIAN RAILWAY MUSEUM

Address: Chappel & Wakes Colne Station, Colchester, Essex CO6 2DS
Telephone Nº: (01206) 242524
Year Formed: 1969
Location of Line: 6 miles west of Colchester on Marks Tey to Sudbury branch
Length of Line: A third of a mile

Nº of Steam Locos: 5   **Other Locos:** 4
Nº of Members: 750
Annual Membership Fee: Adult £20.00; Senior Citizen £15.00
Approx Nº of Visitors P.A.: 40,000
Gauge: Standard
Web site: www.earm.co.uk

GENERAL INFORMATION

Nearest Mainline Station: Chappel & Wakes Colne (adajcent)
Nearest Bus Stop: Wakes Colne Post Office (400 yards)
Car Parking: Free parking at site
Coach Parking: Free parking at site
Souvenir Shop(s): Yes
Food & Drinks: Snacks and drinks are available

SPECIAL INFORMATION

The museum has the most comprehensive collection of railway architecture & engineering in the region. The railway also has a miniature railway that usually operates on steam days.

OPERATING INFORMATION

Opening Times: Open daily 10.00am to 4.30pm. Steam days open from 11.00am to 4.30pm. Closed on Christmas Day and Boxing Day.
Steam Working: Steam days are held every month from April to September and also in October and December. Bank Holidays are also Steam days. Check the web site for further details.
Prices: Adult £5.00 static viewing; £8.00 Steam
Child £2.50 static viewing; £4.00 Steam
O.A.P. £4.25 static viewing; £7.00 Steam
Family £10.00 static viewing; £20.00 Steam
Children under the age of 4 are admitted free of charge. A 10% discount is available for bookings for more than 10 people. A 10% discount is also available for visitors who visit using Mainline trains!

Detailed Directions by Car:
From North & South: Turn off the A12 south west of Colchester onto the A1124 (formerly the A604). The Museum is situated just off the A1124; From West: Turn off the A120 just before Marks Tey (signposted).

EAST KENT RAILWAY

Address: Station Road, Shepherdswell, Dover, Kent CT15 7PD **Telephone N°:** (01304) 832042 **Year Formed:** 1985 **Location of Line:** Between Shepherdswell and Eythorne **Length of Line:** 2 miles	**N° of Steam Locos:** None at present **N° of Other Locos:** 7 + 2 DMUs **N° of Members:** 250 **Annual Membership Fee:** £15.00 (Adult) **Approx N° of Visitors P.A.:** 4,500 **Gauge:** Standard gauge and also 5 inch miniature gauge **Web site:** www.eastkentrailway.co.uk

GENERAL INFORMATION

Nearest Mainline Station: Shepherdswell (50 yards)
Car Parking: Available Shepherdswell and Eythorne
Coach Parking: In adjacent Station Yard
Souvenir Shop(s): Yes
Food & Drinks: Yes

SPECIAL INFORMATION

The East Kent Railway was originally built between 1911 and 1917 to service Tilmanstone Colliery. Closed in the mid-1980's, the railway was re-opened in 1995.

OPERATING INFORMATION

Opening Times: The 2013 operating season opens with a 'Travel for a Pound' day on 21st April and then runs from 5th May until 8th September. Trains run every Sunday and Bank Holiday during this period plus Saturdays in August and during some special events including Halloween and Santa Specials. Contact the railway for further details.
Steam Working: None at present.
Prices: Adult £6.00   Child £3.00
             Senior Citizens £5.00
             Family £15.00 (2 Adults and 2 Children)

Detailed Directions by Car:
From the A2: Take the turning to Shepherdswell and continue to the village. Pass the shop on the left and cross the railway bridge. Take the next left (Station Road) signposted at the traffic lights for the EKR; From the A256: Take the turning for Eythorne at the roundabout on the section between Eastry and Whitfield. Follow the road through Eythorne. Further on you will cross the railway line and enter Shepherdswell. After a few hundred yards take the right turn signposted for the EKR.

East Lancashire Railway

Address: Bolton Street Station, Bury, Lancashire BL9 0EY
Telephone Nº: (0161) 764-7790
Year Formed: 1968
Location of Line: Heywood, Bury and Rawtenstall
Length of Line: 12 miles

Nº of Steam Locos: 14
Nº of Other Locos: 16
Nº of Members: 4,500
Annual Membership Fee: £19.00
Approx Nº of Visitors P.A.: 110,000
Gauge: Standard
Web site: www.eastlancsrailway.org.uk

GENERAL INFORMATION

Nearest Mainline Station: Manchester (then Metro Link to Bury)
Nearest Bus Station: ¼ mile
Car Parking: Adjacent
Coach Parking: Adjacent
Souvenir Shop(s): Yes
Food & Drinks: Yes

SPECIAL INFORMATION

Originally opened in 1846, the East Lancashire Railway was re-opened in 1987.

OPERATING INFORMATION

Opening Times: Every weekend & Bank Holiday 9.00am to 5.00pm. Also Wednesday to Friday from 2nd April to 27th September. A number of special events (including Santa Specials) also run during the year. Please contact the railway for further details.
Steam Working: Most trains are steam-hauled. Saturdays alternate Steam & Diesel. Two engines are in steam on Sundays.
Prices: Adult Return £10.50 – £13.50
Child Return £6.70 – £8.60
Concessionary Return £9.50 – £12.20
Family Return £34.00
Cheaper fares are available for shorter journeys.

Detailed Directions by Car:
From All Parts: Exit the M66 at Junction 2 and take the A56 into Bury. Follow the brown tourist signs and turn right into Bolton Street at the junction with the A58. The station is about 150 yards on the right.

EAST SOMERSET RAILWAY

Address: Cranmore Railway Station, Shepton Mallet, Somerset BA4 4QP
Telephone Nº: (01749) 880417
Year Formed: 1971
Location of Line: Cranmore, off A361 between Frome and Shepton Mallet
Length of Line: 3 miles

Nº of Steam Locos: 5
Nº of Other Locos: 5
Nº of Members: 480
Annual Membership Fee: £15.00
Approx Nº of Visitors P.A.: 20,000
Gauge: Standard
Web site: www.eastsomersetrailway.com

GENERAL INFORMATION

Nearest Mainline Station: Castle Cary (10 miles)
Nearest Bus Station: Shepton Mallet (3 miles)
Car Parking: Space for 100 cars available
Coach Parking: Yes
Souvenir Shop(s): Yes
Food & Drinks: Yes

SPECIAL INFORMATION

Footplate experience courses available – phone (01749) 880417 for further details.

E-mail: info@eastsomersetrailway.com

OPERATING INFORMATION

Opening Times: Complex, Museum and Engine Sheds open daily from April to December and Tuesdays, Thursdays, Saturdays, January to March. Closed on Mondays and Wednesdays in November.
Steam Working: 2013 dates: Weekends and Bank Holidays from March to October, Wednesdays from 5th June to 25th September and Thursdays in July, August and September. Santa Specials run on some December weekends. Special events on other dates. Open 10.00am to 4.00pm (5.30pm in the Summer).
Prices: Adult Return £9.00   Child Return £7.00
Senior Citizen Return £8.00   Family Return £28.00

Detailed Directions by Car:
From the North: Take A367/A37 to Shepton Mallet then turn left onto A361 to Frome. Carry on to Shepton Mallet and 9 miles after Frome turn left at Cranmore; From the South: Take A36 to Frome bypass then A361 to Cranmore; From the West: Take A371 from Wells to Shepton Mallet, then A361 to Frome (then as above).

ECCLESBOURNE VALLEY RAILWAY

Address: Station Road, Coldwell Street, Wirksworth   DE4 4FB
Telephone Nº: (01629) 823076
Year Formed: 2000
Location of Line: Wirksworth to Duffield
Length of Line: 8½ miles

Nº of Steam Locos: 4 (2 operational)
Nº of Other Locos: 8 (including DMUs)
Nº of Members: 700+
Annual Membership Fee: £15.00
Approx Nº of Visitors P.A.: 25,000
Gauge: Standard
Web site: www.e-v-r.com

GENERAL INFORMATION

Nearest Mainline Station: Duffield (adjacent)
Nearest Bus Station: Derby (13 miles)
Car Parking: Available at the Station
Coach Parking: Available at Wirksworth Station
Souvenir Shop(s): Yes
Food & Drinks: Yes

SPECIAL INFORMATION

The line has been restored section by section and the Railway opened all 8½ miles in April 2011.

OPERATING INFORMATION

Opening Times: 2013 dates: Saturdays, Sundays and Bank Holidays from 2nd March to 27th October, Tuesdays from 2nd April to 24th September and Thursdays from 25th July to 29th August. The first departure from Wirksworth is at 10.20am and the first departure from Duffield is at 11.10am. Trains then run every two hours until the last service at 5.10pm.
Steam Working: Some services from 4th May to 19th May and 20th July to 1st September (not Tuesdays). Please contact the railway for further details.
Prices: Adult Day Rover £12.00
　　　　　　Child Day Rover £6.00
　　　　　　Concessions Day Rover £10.00
　　　　　　Family Day Rover £29.00
Note: Prices vary depending on journey length.

Detailed Directions by Car:
From All Parts: Exit the M1 at Junction 26 and take the A610 Ambergate then the A6 to Whatstandwell. Turn left onto the B5035 to Wirksworth and the station is at the bottom of the hill as you enter the town.

ELSECAR HERITAGE RAILWAY

Address: Wath Road, Elsecar, Barnsley, S74 8HJ
Telephone Nº: (01226) 746746
Year Formed: 1997
Location of Line: Elsecar, near Barnsley
Length of Line: 1 mile

Nº of Steam Locos: 5
Nº of Other Locos: 2
Nº of Members: Approximately 60
Annual Membership Fee: £15.00
Approx Nº of Visitors P.A.: 20,000
Gauge: Standard
Web site: www.elsecarrailway.co.uk

GENERAL INFORMATION

Nearest Mainline Station: Elsecar
Nearest Bus Station: Barnsley
Car Parking: Large free car park at the site
Coach Parking: At the site
Souvenir Shop(s): Yes
Food & Drinks: Yes

SPECIAL INFORMATION

The Railway is based at the Elsecar Heritage Centre which is an antiques and craft centre with a wide range of displays and special events.

OPERATING INFORMATION

Opening Times: The Heritage Centre is open daily from 10.00am to 5.00pm throughout the year (but closed between 25th December and 2nd January). Trains run on Sundays, Bank Holidays from Easter through to Christmas. Hourly services operate from 12.00pm to 4.00pm.
Steam Working: Some services are diesel-hauled with regular steaming during the Summer months. Please phone for further details.
Prices: Adults £5.00   Children £2.50
               Senior Citizens £3.00
Admission to the site is free of charge except for during Special Events.

Detailed Directions by Car:
From All Parts: Exit the M1 at Junction 36 and follow the brown 'Elsecar Heritage' signs taking the A6135 for approximately 2 miles. Turn left onto Broad Carr Road for just under a mile, then right onto Armroyd Lane and right again onto Fitzwilliam Street. Free visitor car parking is available on Wentworth Road off the junction of Fitzwilliam Street and Wath Road.

EMBSAY & BOLTON ABBEY STEAM RAILWAY

Address: Bolton Abbey Station, Bolton Abbey, Skipton, N. Yorkshire BD23 6AF	**Nº of Steam Locos:** 14
Telephone Nº: (01756) 710614	**Nº of Other Locos:** 12
Year Formed: 1968	**Nº of Members:** 800
Location of Line: 2 miles east of Skipton	**Annual Membership Fee:** £15.00
Length of Line: 4½ miles	**Approx Nº of Visitors P.A.:** 105,000
	Gauge: Standard

GENERAL INFORMATION

Nearest Mainline Station: Skipton (2 miles), Ilkley (3 miles)
Nearest Bus Station: Skipton (2 miles), Ilkley (3 mls)
Car Parking: Large car park at both Stations
Coach Parking: Large coach park at both Stations
Souvenir Shop(s): Yes
Food & Drinks: Yes – Cafe + Buffet cars

SPECIAL INFORMATION

The line extension to Bolton Abbey opened in 1998.

Web site: www.embsayboltonabbeyrailway.org.uk

OPERATING INFORMATION

Opening Times: Every Sunday throughout the year. Weekends from Easter to the end of October and daily in the summer season until early September. Tuesdays in April, May, June, July, September and October. Santa Specials run on December weekends.
Steam Working: Steam trains depart Embsay Station at 10.30am, 12.00pm, 1.30pm, 3.00pm and 4.30pm on most days during the Main Season. Contact the railway for further details.
Prices: Adult Return £10.00
Child Return £5.00
Family Ticket £25.00 (2 adult + 2 children)
Different fares may apply on special event days.

Detailed Directions by Car:
From All Parts: Embsay Station is off the A59 Skipton bypass by the Harrogate Road. Bolton Abbey Station is off the A59 at Bolton Abbey.

EPPING ONGAR RAILWAY

Address: Ongar Station, Ongar, Essex, CM5 9BN	**Nº of Steam Locos**: 4
Telephone Nº: (01277) 365200	**Nº of Other Locos**: 6
Year Formed: 2004	**Nº of Members**: 460
Location of Line: Epping to Ongar	**Approx Nº of Visitors P.A.**: 25,000
Length of Line: 6 miles	**Gauge**: Standard gauge
	Web site: www.eorailway.co.uk

GENERAL INFORMATION

Nearest Mainline Station: Epping L.U.L. (6½ miles)
Nearest Bus Station: Epping (6½ miles)
Car Parking: Limited free parking at Ongar Station and plenty of spaces at Epping Station. There is no parking whatsoever at North Weald Station.
Coach Parking: By arrangement only
Souvenir Shop(s): Yes
Food & Drinks: Available

SPECIAL INFORMATION

A frequent heritage bus service (number 339) runs from Epping Tube Station to the railway every operating day. A further bus service (number 396) runs from Harlow bus station on selected dates.

OPERATING INFORMATION

Opening Times: Weekends and Bank Holidays from Easter to December and also on Mondays and Fridays during the summer school holidays.
Steam Working: Most operating days.
Prices: Adults £13.00
Children £7.00
Senior Citizens £11.00
Family Ticket £34.00

Detailed Directions by Car:
For North Weald Station: Exit the M11 at Junction 7 and follow the A414 towards Chelmsford and North Weald. Take the 3rd exit at the 2nd roundabout ('The Talbot' pub on the left) and follow the road into North Weald village. Station Road is on the left just after leaving the village. For Ongar Station: Exit the M11 at Junction 7 and follow the A414 towards Chelmsford and North Weald. Follow the road for approximately 5 miles going straight on at two roundabouts. At the 3rd roundabout (BP garage on the left) take the third exit towards Ongar. Epping Ongar Railway is located approximately on the right hand side after approximately 400 yards.

FOXFIELD STEAM RAILWAY

Address: Caverswall Road Station, Blythe Bridge, Stoke-on-Trent, Staffs. ST11 9EA
Telephone Nº: (01782) 396210
Year Formed: 1967
Location of Line: Blythe Bridge
Length of Line: 3½ miles
Gauge: Standard

Nº of Steam Locos: 22
Nº of Other Locos: 15
Nº of Members: Over 300
Annual Membership Fee: Adult £12.00; Junior £6.00; Family £20.00
Approx Nº of Visitors P.A.: 25,000
Web site: www.foxfieldrailway.co.uk

GENERAL INFORMATION

Nearest Mainline Station: Blythe Bridge (¼ mile)
Nearest Bus Station: Hanley (5 miles)
Car Parking: Space for 300 cars available
Coach Parking: Space for 6 coaches available
Souvenir Shop(s): Yes
Food & Drinks: Yes – Buffet and Real Ale Bar

SPECIAL INFORMATION

The Railway is a former Colliery railway built in 1893 to take coal from Foxfield Colliery. It has the steepest Standard Gauge adhesion worked gradient in the UK and freight trains can be seen on these gradients during the annual Steam Gala in July.

OPERATING INFORMATION

Opening Times: 2013 dates: Sundays & Bank Holiday Mondays from 1st April to 27th October. Also Wednesdays from 24th July to 28th August and weekends in December. Open 11.00am to 5.00pm.
Steam Working: 11.30am, 1.00pm, 2.30pm and 4.00pm although Special Event days also run trains at earlier times.
Prices: Adult Tickets – £7.50
Child Tickets – £3.00 (3-16 years old)
Senior Citizen Tickets – £5.50
Fares may vary on special event days.

Detailed Directions by Car:
From South: Exit M6 at Junction 14 onto the A34 to Stone then the A520 to Meir and the A50 to Blythe Bridge; From North: Exit M6 at Junction 15 then the A500 to Stoke-on-Trent and the A50 to Blythe Bridge; From East: Take the A50 to Blythe Bridge. Once in Blythe Bridge, turn by the Mainline crossing.

GLOUCESTERSHIRE WARWICKSHIRE RAILWAY

Address: The Station, Toddington, Cheltenham, Gloucestershire GL54 5DT
Telephone Nº: (01242) 621405
Year Formed: 1981
Location of Line: 5 miles south of Broadway, Worcestershire, near the A46
Length of Line: 12 miles

Nº of Steam Locos: 11
Nº of Other Locos: 17
Nº of Members: 3,500
Annual Membership Fee: £16.00 (Adult)
Approx Nº of Visitors P.A.: 70,000
Gauge: Standard and Narrow gauge
Web site: www.gwsr.com

GENERAL INFORMATION

Nearest Mainline Station: Cheltenham Spa or Ashchurch
Nearest Bus Station: Cheltenham
Car Parking: Parking available at Toddington, Winchcombe & Cheltenham Racecourse Stations
Coach Parking: Parking available as above
Souvenir Shop(s): Yes   **Food & Drinks:** Yes

SPECIAL INFORMATION

The full length of the line has now reopened following the rebuilding of an embankment north of Winchcombe.

OPERATING INFORMATION

Opening Times: Weekends and Bank Holidays from February to December. Also during most weekdays from June to October. Trains run from 10.30am to 5.00pm
Steam Working: Most weekends and on Wednesdays during the Summer school holidays.
Prices: Adult Day Rover £15.00
Child Day Rover £6.00
Senior Citizen Day Rover £14.00
Family Ticket Day Rover £38.00
(2 Adults + 3 Children)
Under 5's travel free of charge apart from on some Special Event days.

Detailed Directions by Car:
Toddington is 11 miles north east of Cheltenham, 5 miles south of Broadway just off the B4632 (old A46). Exit the M5 at Junction 9 towards Stow-on-the-Wold for the B4632. The Railway is clearly visible from the B4632.

GREAT CENTRAL RAILWAY

Address: Great Central Station, Great Central Road, Loughborough, Leicestershire LE11 1RW **Telephone No:** (01509) 632323 **Year Formed:** 1969 **Location of Line:** From Loughborough to Leicester	**Length of Line:** 8 miles **No of Steam Locos:** 10 **No of Other Locos:** 11 **No of Members:** 5,000 **Annual Membership Fee:** £20.00 **Approx No of Visitors P.A.:** 100,000 **Gauge:** Standard

GENERAL INFORMATION

Nearest Mainline Station: Loughborough (1 mile)
Nearest Bus Station: Loughborough (½ mile)
Car Parking: Street parking outside the Station
Coach Parking: Car parks at Quorn & Woodhouse, Rothley and Leicester North
Souvenir Shop(s): Yes
Food & Drinks: Yes – Buffet or Restaurant cars are usually available for snacks or other meals

Web site: www.gcrailway.co.uk

SPECIAL INFORMATION

The aim of the GCR is to recreate the experience of British main line railway operation during the best years of steam locomotives.

OPERATING INFORMATION

Opening Times: 2013 dates: Weekends throughout the year, Wednesdays from June to September and Tuesdays and Thursdays 16th July to 29th August. Santa Specials in December and other dates throughout the year. Contact the railway for details.
Steam Working: Weekends, Bank Holidays and some Special Events throughout the year.
Prices: Adult Day ticket £15.00
Child Day ticket £9.00
Senior Citizen Day ticket £13.00
Family Day Ticket £34 (2 adults + 3 children)

Detailed Directions by Car:
Great Central Road is on the South East side of Loughborough and is clearly signposted from the A6 Leicester Road and A60 Nottingham Road.

GREAT CENTRAL RAILWAY (NOTTINGHAM)

Address: Nottingham Transport Heritage
Centre, Mere Way, Ruddington,
Nottingham   NG11 6NX
Telephone No: (0115) 940-5705
Fax No: (0115) 940-5905
Year Formed: 1990 (Opened in 1994)
Location of Line: Ruddington to
Loughborough Junction

Length of Line: 9 miles
No of Steam Locos: 6
No of Other Locos: 10
No of Members: 750
Annual Membership Fee: £14.00
Approx No of Visitors P.A.: 15,000
Gauge: Standard
Web site: www.gcrn.co.uk

GENERAL INFO

Nearest Mainline Station:
Nottingham (5 miles)
Nearest Bus Station: Bus service
from Nottingham to Ruddington
Car Parking: Free parking at site
Coach Parking: Free parking at site
Souvenir Shop(s): Yes
Food & Drinks: Yes

SPECIAL INFORMATION

The Heritage Centre covers an area
of more than eleven acres and is set
within the Rushcliffe Country Park
in Ruddington. Trains run to
Loughborough Junction or
Rushcliffe Halt.

OPERATING INFO

Opening Times: Sundays and Bank
Holidays plus some Saturdays from
Easter until October. Open 10.45am
to 5.00pm. Also open for Santa
Specials on December weekends.
Steam Working: Steam service runs
from 11.30am
Prices: Adult £8.00 – £10.00
Child £4.00 – £5.00
Senior Citizens £7.00–£9.00
Family £20.00 – £25.00
(2 adults + 3 children)
Note: Prices vary depending on the
journey length and all prices shown
above are for unlimited day rover
tickets.

Detailed Directions by Car:
From All Parts: The centre is situated off the A60 Nottingham to Loughborough Road and is signposted just
south of the traffic lights at Ruddington.

GWILI RAILWAY

Address: Bronwydd Arms Station, Bronwydd Arms, Carmarthen SA33 6HT
Telephone Nº: (01267) 238213
E-mail: company@gwili-railway.co.uk
Year Formed: 1975
Location of Line: Near Carmarthen, South Wales
Length of Line: 2½ miles

Nº of Steam Locos: 5
Nº of Other Locos: 6
Nº of Members: 900 shareholders, 450 Society members
Annual Membership Fee: £15.00
Approx Nº of Visitors P.A.: 28,000
Gauge: Standard
Web site: www.gwili-railway.co.uk

GENERAL INFORMATION

Nearest Mainline Station: Carmarthen (3 miles)
Nearest Bus Station: Carmarthen (3 miles)
Car Parking: Free parking at Bronwydd Arms
Coach Parking: Free parking at Bronwydd Arms
Souvenir Shop(s): Yes
Food & Drinks: Yes

SPECIAL INFORMATION

Gwili Railway was the first Standard Gauge preserved railway in West Wales. There is a riverside picnic area and Miniature railway at Llwyfan Cerrig Station and there is a Signal Box Museum at Bronwydd Arms.

OPERATING INFORMATION

Opening Times: Wednesday and Thursday from May to July and also in September and October. Daily from the end of July to the end of August. Sundays in October and Santa Specials run on December weekends. Please phone or check the website for further details about Special Events.

Steam Working: All advertised trains are steam hauled. Trains run from 10.30am to 4.00pm in high season and 10.30am to 2.50pm at other times.

Prices: Adult £9.00
Child £3.00 (Under-2s ride free of charge)
Family £20.00 (2 adults + up to 2 children)
Senior Citizens £8.00

Note: Discounts are available for larger groups (10+).

Detailed Directions by Car:
The Railway is three miles North of Carmarthen – signposted off the A484 Carmarthen to Cardigan Road.

HEAD OF STEAM – DARLINGTON RAILWAY MUSEUM

Address: North Road Station, Darlington, Co. Durham   DL3 6ST
Telephone Nº: (01325) 460532
Year Formed: 1975
Location of Line: Adjacent to North Road Station
Length of Line: ¼ mile

Nº of Steam Locos: 4
Nº of Other Locos: None
Nº of Members: 800 family memberships
Annual Membership Fee: £10.00 (adult) £15.00 (family);   £10.00 (senior)
Approx Nº of Visitors P.A.: 33,500
Gauge: Standard
Web site: www.head-of-steam.co.uk

GENERAL INFORMATION

Nearest Mainline Station: North Road (adjacent)
Nearest Bus Station: Darlington (1 mile)
Car Parking: Free parking at site
Coach Parking: Free parking at site
Souvenir Shop(s): Yes
Food & Drinks: Cafe open 11.00am to 2.00pm (until 3.00pm at weekends).

SPECIAL INFORMATION

The museum is an 1842 station on the route of the Stockton and Darlington Railway and is devoted to the Railways of north-east England.

OPERATING INFORMATION

Opening Times: The Museum is open daily throughout the year but is closed every Monday. from April to September and every Monday and Tuesday from October to March. Also closed on Christmas Day, Boxing Day and New Year's Day. Open 10.00am to 4.00pm April to September and from 11.00am to 3.30pm from October to March.
Steam Working: At various Special events throughout the year – please phone for details.
Prices: Adult £4.95
Child £3.00 (ages 5 and under enter free)
Senior Citizen £3.75
Family Ticket £10.00
(2 adults and up to 4 children)

Detailed Directions by Car:
From Darlington Town Centre: Follow the A167 north for about ¾ mile then turn left immediately before the Railway bridge; From A1(M): Exit at Junction 59 then follow A167 towards Darlington and turn right after passing under the Railway bridge.

HELSTON RAILWAY

Address: Trevarno Farm, Prospidnick, Helston, Cornwall TR13 0RY	**N° of Steam Locos**: None
Contact Telephone N°: 07901 977597	**N° of Other Locos**: 2 (plus 1 DMU)
E-mail: manager@helstonrailway.co.uk	**N° of Members**: 1,000 approximately
Year Formed: 2002	**Annual Membership Fee**: £10.00
Location: Trevarno Farm, Helston	**Approx N° of Visitors P.A.**: Not known
	Gauge: Standard
Length of Line: 1 mile	**Web site**: www.helstonrailway.co.uk

GENERAL INFORMATION

Nearest Mainline Station: Camborne (6 miles)
Nearest Bus Station: Camborne
Car Parking: Free parking at Trevano Farm
Coach Parking: At Trevano Farm
Souvenir Shop(s): Yes
Food & Drinks: Light refreshments are available

SPECIAL INFORMATION

The railway is operated by the Helston Railway Preservation Society which was formed in 2002. The long term aim is to re-open a three mile section of the old Helston branch line running through the Cornish countryside between Nancegollan and Helston Water-Ma-Trout.

OPERATING INFORMATION

Opening Times: Every Thursday, Sunday and Bank Holiday from Easter to November. Open from 10.30am to 4.00pm and also for some Evening Specials during the summer months.
Steam Working: Brake Van rides only at present but the railway hopes to have visiting steam locos on certain dates during 2013. Please contact the railway for further information.
Prices: Adults £5.00 (Brake Van rides)
Children £3.00 (Brake Van rides)
(Under-5s ride free of charge)
Shunter Footplate Rides £10.00 (Adults)
Note: Access to the railway is available via Trevarno Farm car park.

Detailed Directions by Car:
The railway is situated 1½ miles to the north of Helston, just off the B3303 between Crowntown and Nancegollan.

ISLE OF WIGHT STEAM RAILWAY

Address: The Railway Station, Havenstreet, Near Ryde, Isle of Wight PO33 4DS
Telephone Nº: (01983) 882204
Year Formed: 1971 (re-opened)
Location: Smallbrook Junction to Wootton
Length of Line: 5 miles
Nº of Steam Locos: 11

Nº of Other Locos: 3
Nº of Members: 1,450
Annual Membership Fee: £20.00
Approx Nº of Visitors P.A.: 110,000
Gauge: Standard
Talking Timetable: (01983) 884343
Web site: www.iwsteamrailway.co.uk

GENERAL INFORMATION

Nearest Mainline Station: Smallbrook Junction (direct interchange)
Nearest Bus: From Ryde & Newport direct
Car Parking: Free parking at Havenstreet & Wootton Stations
Coach Parking: Free at Havenstreet Station
Souvenir Shop(s): Yes – at Havenstreet Station
Food & Drinks: Yes – at Havenstreet Station

SPECIAL INFORMATION

The IWSR uses mostly Victorian & Edwardian locomotives and carriages to recreate the atmosphere of an Isle of Wight branch line railway.

OPERATING INFORMATION

Opening Times: 2013 dates: Most days in April and May then daily from 25th May to 29th September (closed on 20th, 21st, & 27th September). Open on Wednesdays, Thursdays and Sundays in October and on dates in November and December. Please contact the railway for further information.
Steam Working: 10.30am to 4.00pm (depending on the Station)
Prices: Adult Return £10.50
　　　　　Child Return £5.50 (Under-5s travel free)
　　　　　Family Return £26.50
　　　　　　　　　(2 adults + 2 children)
Note: First Class fares are higher than prices shown

Detailed Directions by Car:
To reach the Isle of Wight head for the Ferry ports at Lymington, Southampton or Portsmouth. From all parts of the Isle of Wight, head for Havenstreet (which is located 3 miles from Ryde and 3 miles from Newport), and follow the brown tourist signs.

KEIGHLEY & WORTH VALLEY RAILWAY

Address: The Station, Haworth, Keighley, West Yorkshire   BD22 8NJ
Telephone Nº: (01535) 645214 (enquiries)
Year Formed: 1962 (Line re-opened 1968)
Location of Line: From Keighley southwards through Haworth to Oxenhope
Length of Line: 4¾ miles

Nº of Steam Locos: 30
Nº of Other Locos: 10
Members: 4,500 (350 working members)
Annual Membership Fee: Adult £21.00; Adult life membership £410.00
Approx Nº of Visitors P.A.: 120,000
Gauge: Standard
Web Site: www.kwvr.co.uk

GENERAL INFORMATION

Nearest Mainline Station: Keighley (adjacent)
Nearest Bus Station: Keighley (5 minutes walk)
Car Parking: Parking at Keighley, Ingrow, Haworth (charged) and Oxenhope
Coach Parking: At Ingrow & Oxenhope (phone in advance)
Souvenir Shop(s): Yes – at Keighley, Oxenhope & Haworth (whose shop also sells books/DVDs)
Food & Drinks: Yes – at Keighley & Oxenhope when trains run.

OPERATING INFORMATION

Opening Times: 2013 dates: Weekends & Bank Holidays throughout the year. Daily from 25th May to 8th September. Also open during Easter, Whit and February and October School holidays and from 26th to 31st December.
Steam Working: Early trains are Diesel; Steam runs from mid-morning on all operating days including the 4 weekends prior to Christmas when Santa Specials operate (pre-booking necessary for these).
Prices: Adult Return £10.00   (£15.00 Day Rover)
        Child Return £5.00   (£7.50 Day Rover)
        Family Day Rover £35.00 (2 adult + 3 child)
        Concession Day Rover £12.50

Detailed Directions by Car:
Exit the M62 at Junction 26 and take the M606 to its' end. Follow the ring-road signs around Bradford to Shipley. Take the A650 through Bingley to Keighley and follow the brown tourist signs to the railway. Alternatively, take the A6033 from Hebden Bridge to Oxenhope and follow the brown signs to Oxenhope or Haworth Stations.

THE KEITH & DUFFTOWN RAILWAY

Address: Dufftown Station, Dufftown, Banffshire, AB55 4BA
Telephone Nº: (01340) 821181
Year Formed: 2000
Location of Line: Keith to Dufftown
Length of Line: 11 miles

Nº of Steam Locos: None at present
Nº of Other Locos: 2 DMU + 2 shunters
Nº of Members: Approximately 400
Annual Membership Fee: Adult £13.00
Approx Nº of Visitors P.A.: Not known
Gauge: Standard
Web: www.keith-dufftown-railway.co.uk

GENERAL INFORMATION

Nearest Mainline Station: Keith (½ mile)
Nearest Bus Station: Elgin (Bus routes travel to both Keith and Dufftown)
Car Parking: Available at both Stations
Coach Parking: Available at both Stations
Souvenir Shop(s): Yes – at Keith Town Station
Food & Drinks: Available at Dufftown Station

SPECIAL INFORMATION

The Keith and Dufftown Railway is an eleven mile line linking the World's Malt Whisky Capital, Dufftown, to the market town of Keith. The line, which was reopened by volunteers during 2000 and 2001, passes through some of Scotland's most picturesque scenery, with forest and farmland, lochs and glens, castles and distilleries.

OPERATING INFORMATION

Opening Times: Weekends from Easter until the end of September and also on Fridays in June, July and August. Trains depart Dufftown from 11.25am until 4.40pm.
Steam Working: None at present
Prices: Adult Return £10.00
Child Return £5.00
Senior Citizen Return £8.00
Family Return £26.00
Note: Shorter journeys are cheaper.

Detailed Directions by Car:
Keith Town Station is located in Keith, on the A96 Aberdeen to Inverness Road; Dufftown Station is about 1 mile to the north of the Dufftown Town Centre just off the A941 road to Elgin.

KENT & EAST SUSSEX RAILWAY

Address: Tenterden Town Station, Tenterden, Kent   TN30 6HE
Telephone Nº: (01580) 765155
Year Formed: 1974
Location of Line: Tenterden, Kent to Bodiam, East Sussex
Length of Line: 10½ miles

Nº of Steam Locos: 12
Nº of Other Locos: 6
Nº of Members: 2,100
Annual Membership Fee: £23.00
Approx Nº of Visitors P.A.: 99,000
Gauge: Standard
Web site: www.kesr.org.uk

GENERAL INFORMATION

Nearest Mainline Station: Headcorn (8 miles)
Nearest Bus Station: Tenterden
Car Parking: Free parking available at Tenterden Town and Northiam Stations
Coach Parking: Tenterden & Northiam
Souvenir Shop(s): Yes
Food & Drinks: Yes

SPECIAL INFORMATION

Built as Britain's first light railway, the K&ESR opened in 1900 and was epitomised by sharp curved and steep gradients and to this day retains a charm and atmosphere all of its own.

OPERATING INFORMATION

Opening Times: From February to October and in December. The return journey time is 1 hour 55 minutes. Please phone the 24 hour talking-timetable for precise operating information: (01580) 762943
Steam Working: Every operational day
Prices: Adult Ticket – £15.00
　　　　　Child Ticket – £10.00
　　　　　Senior Citizen Ticket – £14.00
　　　　　Family Ticket – £42.00
　　　　　(2 adults + 3 children or 1 adult + 4 children)
Note: The prices shown above are for Day Rover tickets which allow unlimited travel on the day of purchase.

Detailed Directions by Car:
From London and Kent Coast: Travel to Ashford (M20) then take the A28 to Tenterden; From Sussex Coast: Take A28 from Hastings to Northiam.

LAKESIDE & HAVERTHWAITE RAILWAY

Address: Haverthwaite Station, near Ulverston, Cumbria LA12 8AL	**Nº of Steam Locos**: 8
Telephone Nº: (015395) 31594	**Nº of Other Locos**: 6
E-mail: info@lakesiderailway.co.uk	**Nº of Members**: 250
Year Formed: 1973	**Annual Membership Fee**: £12.00 Adult, £6.00 Juniors
Location of Line: Haverthwaite to Lakeside	**Approx Nº of Visitors P.A.**: 170,000
Length of Line: 3½ miles	**Gauge**: Standard
	Web site: www.lakesiderailway.co.uk

GENERAL INFORMATION

Nearest Mainline Station: Ulverston (7 miles)
Nearest Bus Station: Haverthwaite (100 yards)
Car Parking: Plenty of spaces – Charges from £1.00
Coach Parking: Free parking at site
Souvenir Shop(s): Yes
Food & Drinks: Yes

SPECIAL INFORMATION

Tickets which include train ride followed by a cruise on Lake Windermere or a visit to the Aquarium of the Lakes are also available from the Railway.

OPERATING INFORMATION

Opening Times: 2013 dates: Daily from 28th March to 3rd November inclusive. Also open for Santa Specials on 1st, 7th, 8th, 14th, 15th, 21st & 22nd December. A number of other Special Events run throughout the year. Please contact the railway for further information.
Steam Working: Daily from morning to late afternoon.
Prices: Adult Return £6.40   Single £3.80
     Child Return £3.20   Single £2.50
     Family Ticket £17.50
Note: Prices vary for Special Events and individual fares apply for combined tickets including other attractions.

Detailed Directions by Car:
From All Parts: Exit the M6 at Junction 36 and follow the brown tourist signs.

THE LAVENDER LINE

Address: Isfield Station, Isfield, near Uckfield, East Sussex   TN22 5XB
Telephone Nº: (01825) 750515
Year Formed: 1992
Location of Line: East Sussex between Lewes and Uckfield
Length of Line: 1 mile

Nº of Steam Locos: 1
Nº of Other Locos: 3 + DEMU
Nº of Members: Approximately 400
Annual Membership Fee: £15.00
Approx Nº of Visitors P.A.: 12,500
Gauge: Standard
Web site: www.lavender-line.co.uk

GENERAL INFORMATION

Nearest Mainline Station: Uckfield (3 miles)
Nearest Bus Station: Uckfield (3 miles)
Car Parking: Free parking at site
Coach Parking: Can cater for coach parties – please contact the Railway.
Souvenir Shop: Yes
Food & Drinks: Yes – Cinders Buffet

SPECIAL INFORMATION

Isfield Station has been restored as a Southern Railway country station complete with the original L.B.S.C.R. signalbox.

OPERATING INFORMATION

Opening Times: Sundays throughout the year plus a number of other Special Event dates including Santa Specials in December. Please contact the railway for further details.
Steam Working: The first and last Sundays of the month from April to October inclusive plus some other dates. Contact the railway for further details.
Prices: Adult £9.00   (£8.00 on Diesel days)
Child £6.00   (£5.00 on Diesel days)
Senior Citizen £7.00 (£6.00 on Diesel days)
Family Ticket £28.00   (£25.00 Diesel days)
(2 adults + 3 children)
All tickets offer unlimited rides on the day of issue and prices may vary on special event days.

Detailed Directions by Car::
From All Parts: Isfield is just off the A26 midway between Lewes and Uckfield.

LINCOLNSHIRE WOLDS RAILWAY

Address: The Railway Station, Ludborough, Lincolnshire DN36 5SQ **Telephone Nº**: (01507) 363881 **Year Formed**: 1979 **Location of Line**: Ludborough – off the A16(T) between Grimsby and Louth **Length of Line**: 1½ miles	**Nº of Steam Locos**: 4 **Other Locos**: 7 **Nº of Members**: 400+ **Annual Membership Fee**: £30.00 Family, £15.00 Adult, £10.00 Senior Citizen **Approx Nº of Visitors P.A.**: 9,000 **Gauge**: Standard **Web**: www.lincolnshirewoldsrailway.co.uk

GENERAL INFORMATION

Nearest Mainline Station: Grimsby (8 miles)
Nearest Bus Stop: Ludborough (½ mile)
Car Parking: Available at Ludborough Station only
Coach Parking: Space for 1 coach only
Souvenir Shop(s): Yes
Food & Drinks: Yes

SPECIAL INFORMATION

The buildings and facilities at Ludborough have been completed and short steam trips commenced in 1998. A line extension to North Thoresby (1½ miles) is now open.

E-mail: contact@lincolnshirewoldsrailway.co.uk

OPERATING INFORMATION

Opening Times: 2013 dates: 10th, 30th & 31st March; 1st, 14th & 28th April; 5th, 6th, 19th, 26th & 27th May; 2nd & 16th June; 7th, 21st & 31st July; 4th, 7th, 11th, 14th, 18th, 21st, 25th, 26th & 28th August; 7th, 8th & 29th September; 13th, 23rd & 27th October; 2nd November; 1st, 7th, 8th, 14th & 15th December for Santa Specials. Also open 1st January 2014. Please note that advance bookings are essential for Santa Specials.
Steam Working: All operating days if possible.
Prices: Adults £7.00   Children £4.00
              Senior Citizens £5.00
              Family £18.00 (2 adults + 4 children)
Different fares may apply at Special Events.
Prices include unlimited rides throughout the day.

Detailed Directions by Car:
The Railway is situated near Ludborough, ½ mile off the A16(T) Louth to Grimsby road. Follow the brown tourist signs for ½ mile to Fulstow to reach the station. Do not turn into Ludborough but stay on the bypass.

LLANGOLLEN RAILWAY

Address: The Station, Abbey Road, Llangollen, Denbighshire LL20 8SN
Telephone Nº: (01978) 860979
Year Formed: 1975
Location of Line: Valley of the River Dee from Llangollen to Carrog
Length of Line: 7½ miles at present

Nº of Steam Locos: 14   **Other Locos**: 13
Nº of Members: 1,400
Annual Membership Fee: Adult £18.00; Family £25.00; Junior (under-16) £10.00
Approx Nº of Visitors P.A.: 110,000
Gauge: Standard
Web Site: www.llangollen-railway.co.uk

GENERAL INFORMATION

Nearest Mainline Station: Ruabon (6 miles)
Nearest Bus Station: Wrexham (12 miles)
Car Parking: Llangollen Royal International Pavilion (SatNav post code: LL20 8SW)
Coach Parking: Market Street car park in town centre (SatNav post code: LL20 8PS)
Souvenir Shop(s): Yes – at Llangollen Station
Food & Drinks: Yes – at Llangollen, Berwyn, Glyndyfrdwy and Carrog Stations.

SPECIAL INFORMATION

The route originally formed part of the line from Ruabon to Barmouth Junction, closed in 1964. The railway has been rebuilt by volunteers since 1975, reopening to Carrog in 1996 and is to be extended 2½ miles to Corwen by Autumn 2013.

OPERATING INFORMATION

Opening Times: 2013 dates: Services run daily from Easter until early October. Also on weekends in December and for Santa Specials near Christmas.
Steam Working: Phone the Talking timetable number for further details: (01978) 860951
Prices: Adult Day Rover £14.00
Child Day Rover £7.00
Family Day Rover £36.00 (2 adult + 2 child)
Senior Citizen Day Rover £12.00
Note: Tickets for shorter journeys are available.

Detailed Directions by Car:
From South & West: Go via the A5 to Llangollen. At the traffic lights turn into Castle Street to the River bridge; From North & East: Take the A483 to A539 junction and then via Trefor to Llangollen River bridge. The Station is adjacent to the River Dee.

LOCOMOTION – THE NATIONAL RAILWAY MUSEUM AT SHILDON

Address: Locomotion, Shildon, County Durham   DL14 1PQ
Telephone Nº: (01388) 777999
Fax Nº: (01388) 771448
Year Formed: 2004
Location: Shildon, County Durham

Length of Line: Over ½ mile
Nº of Steam Locos: 60 locomotives and other rail vehicles
Approx Nº of Visitors P.A.: 70,000+
Gauge: Standard
Web site: www.nrm.org.uk/locomotion

GENERAL INFORMATION

Nearest Mainline Station: Shildon (adjacent)
Nearest Bus Station: Durham
Car Parking: Available on site
Coach Parking: Available on site
Souvenir Shop(s): Yes
Food & Drinks: Yes

SPECIAL INFORMATION

This extensive site is the first regional branch of the National Railway Museum and houses vehicles from the National Collection in a purpose-built 6,000 square-foot building.

OPERATING INFORMATION

Opening Times: 2013 dates: During the winter months (30th September 2013 to 30th March 2014), The Collection Building will be open on Mondays and Tuesdays only – 10.00am to 4.00pm. Closed between 23rd & 26th December and New Year's Day. The whole site is open daily during the summer (1st April to 29th September) – 10.00am to 5.00pm.
Steam Working: During the Summer School Holidays and on special event days – please contact the museum or check their web site for details.
Prices: Admission to the Museum is free of charge.
Train Rides: Adults £2.50   Concessions £1.25
Adult All Day Ticket £4.50
Child All Day Ticket £2.50

Detailed Directions by Car:
From All Parts: Exit the A1(M) at Junction 58 and take the A68 and the A6072 to Shildon. Follow the Brown tourist signs to Locomotion which is situated ¼ mile to the south-east of the Town Centre.
Drivers using SATNAVs should enter the following post code: DL14 2RE

MANGAPPS RAILWAY MUSEUM

Address: Southminster Road, Burnham-on-Crouch, Essex CM0 8QG
Telephone N°: (01621) 784898
Year Formed: 1989
Location of Line: Mangapps Farm
Length of Line: ¾ mile

N° of Steam Locos: 6
N° of Other Locos: 12
Approx N° of Visitors P.A.: 22,000
Gauge: Standard
Web site: www.mangapps.co.uk
E-mail: mangapps@tiscali.co.uk

GENERAL INFORMATION

Nearest Mainline Station: Burnham-on-Crouch (1 mile)
Nearest Bus Station: –
Car Parking: Ample free parking at site
Coach Parking: Ample free parking at site
Souvenir Shop(s): Yes
Food & Drinks: Yes – drinks and snacks only

SPECIAL INFORMATION

The Railway endeavours to recreate the atmosphere of an East Anglian light railway. It also includes an extensive museum with an emphasis on East Anglian items and signalling.

OPERATING INFORMATION

Opening Times: Closed during January and November, then open every weekend and Bank Holiday (except over Christmas) and daily during August. Santa Specials run during weekends in December. Please contact the railway for details of opening times during the School Holidays and for any other information.
Steam Working: Bank Holiday Sundays and Mondays plus certain other dates. Diesel at other times. Please contact the railway for further details.
Prices: Adult – Steam £8.00; Diesel £7.00
Child – Steam £3.50; Diesel £3.00
Senior Citizen – Steam £7.00; Diesel £6.00
Note: Prices for special events may differ.

Detailed Directions by Car:
From South & West: From M25 take either the A12 or A127 and then the A130 to Rettendon Turnpike and then follow signs to Burnham; From North: From A12 take A414 to Oak Corner then follow signs to Burnham.

THE MIDDLETON RAILWAY

Address: The Station, Moor Road, Hunslet, Leeds LS10 2JQ
Telephone Nº: (0113) 271-0320
Year Formed: 1960
Location of Line: Moor Road to Middleton Park
Length of Line: 1½ miles

Nº of Steam Locos: 20
Nº of Other Locos: 13
Annual Membership Fee: Adults £17.00
Approx Nº of Visitors P.A.: 20,000
Gauge: Standard
Web Site: www.middletonrailway.org.uk

GENERAL INFORMATION

Nearest Mainline Station:
Leeds City (1 mile)
Nearest Bus Station: Leeds (1½ miles)
Car Parking: Free parking at site
Coach Parking: Free parking at site
Souvenir Shop(s): Yes
Food & Drinks: Yes

SPECIAL INFORMATION

The Middleton Railway is the oldest working railway in the world and was established in 1758 by Act of Parliament. The railway is also the first Standard Gauge line to be operated by volunteers and the first revenue-earning steam locomotive ran here in 1812. The railway also hosts a working museum housing a collection of Leeds built locomotives.

OPERATING INFORMATION

Opening Times: 2013 dates: Weekends and Bank Holidays from 30th March to the end of November plus Santa Specials in December. Also open on Wednesdays in August. Services run approximately every 40 minutes from 11.00am to 4.00pm.
Steam Working: Diesels usually operate on Saturdays and on Wednesdays in August. All other services are usually steam-hauled including Santa Specials in December.
Prices: Adult £5.00   Child £2.50
          Family £13.00
                  (2 adults + 3 children)
Tickets provide for unlimited travel on the day of issue. For a full timetable and details of special events, please check the railway's web site or phone 0845 680-1758.
Note: Different prices may apply on Special Event days.

Detailed Directions by Car:
From the South: Take the M621 Northbound and exit at Junction 5. Turn right at the top of the slip road and take the 3rd exit at the roundabout. The Railway is 50 yards on the right; From the West: Take the M621 Southbound and exit at Junction 6. Turn left at the end of the slip road then left again into Moor Road at the next set of traffic lights. Bear right at the mini roundabout and the railway is on the left after 150 yards.

MID-HANTS RAILWAY (WATERCRESS LINE)

Address: The Railway Station, Alresford, Hampshire SO24 9JG
Telephone N°: (01962) 733810 General enquiries; (01962) 734866 Timetable
Year Formed: 1977
Location of Line: Alresford to Alton
Length of Line: 10 miles

N° of Steam Locos: 24 (9 in steam)
N° of Other Locos: 8
N° of Members: 3,500
Annual Membership Fee: Adult £25.00
Approx N° of Visitors P.A.: 150,000
Gauge: Standard
Web Site: www.watercressline.co.uk

Photo courtesy of Matt Allen

GENERAL INFORMATION

Nearest Mainline Station: Alton (adjacent) or Winchester (7 miles)
Nearest Bus Station: Winchester or Alton
Car Parking: Pay and display at Alton and Alresford Stations (Alresford free on Sundays & Bank Holidays)
Coach Parking: By arrangement at Alresford Station
Souvenir Shop(s): At Alresford, Ropley & Alton
Food & Drinks: Yes – Buffet on most trains. 'West Country' buffet at Alresford

SPECIAL INFORMATION

The railway runs through four fully restored stations and has a Loco yard and picnic area at Ropley.

OPERATING INFORMATION

Opening Times: 2013 dates: Weekends and Bank Holidays from January to October plus Tuesday to Thursday from May to the 26th September. Daily during the School holidays. Santa Specials run at weekends and on other dates in December.
Steam Working: All operating days although a Steam/DMU combination is sometimes in service.
Prices: Adult £14.00
Child (ages 2 to 16) £7.00 (Under-2s free)
Family £35.00 (2 adults + 2 children)
Prices shown above are for Day Rover fares.
A discount is available for pre-booked parties of 15 or more people. Write or call for a booking form.

Detailed Directions by Car:
From the East: Take the M25 then A3 and A31 to Alton; From the West: Exit the M3 at Junction 9 and take the A31 to Alresford Station.

MID-NORFOLK RAILWAY

Address: The Railway Station,
Station Road, Dereham NR19 1DF
Telephone Nº: (01362) 690633 or 851723
Year Formed: 1995
Location: East Dereham to Wymondham
Length of Line: 11 miles

Nº of Steam Locos: Visiting locos only
Nº of Other Locos: 9
Nº of Members: 1,000
Annual Membership Fee: £16.00
Approx Nº of Visitors P.A.: 16,000
Gauge: Standard
Web site: www.mnr.org.uk

GENERAL INFORMATION

Nearest Mainline Station: Wymondham (1 mile)
Nearest Bus Station: Wymondham or East
Dereham – each ½ mile away
Car Parking: Available at Dereham Station
Coach Parking: Available at Dereham Station
Souvenir Shop(s): Yes – at Dereham Station
Food & Drinks: Yes – at Dereham Station

SPECIAL INFORMATION

The Mid-Norfolk Railway aims to preserve the
former Great Eastern Railway from Wymondham to
County School. The section from Wymondham to
Dereham was opened to passenger and freight traffic
in May 1999 and clearance work is now complete on
the East Dereham to County School section.

OPERATING INFORMATION

Opening Times: 2013 dates: Weekends and Bank
Holidays from 29th March to 3rd November. Also
on Wednesdays from 1st May to 30th October and
Thursdays from 30th May to 26th September.
Santa Specials run on some dates in December.
Steam Working: Weekends and Bank Holidays
from 8th June to 1st September inclusive with a
visiting Steam locomotive.
Prices: Adult Return £7.00 (Diesel)
Child Return £3.50 (Diesel)
Senior Citizen Return £6.00 (Diesel)
Adult Return £10.00 (Steam days)
Child Return £5.00 (Steam days)
Senior Citizen Return £9.00 (Steam days)

Detailed Directions by Car:
From All Parts: From the A47 bypass, turn into Dereham and follow the signs for the Town Centre. Turn right at
the BP Garage – look out for the brown tourist signs – you will see the Station on your right.

MID-SUFFOLK LIGHT RAILWAY MUSEUM

Address: Brockford Station, Wetheringsett, Suffolk   IP14 5PW
Telephone Nº: (01449) 766899
Year Formed: 1990
Location of Line: Wetheringsett, Suffolk
Length of Line: ¼ mile

Nº of Steam Locos: 2 (1 operational)
Nº of Other Locos: 1
Nº of Members: 400
Annual Membership Fee: £12.00
Approx Nº of Visitors P.A.: 2,000
Gauge: Standard
Web site: www.mslr.org.uk

GENERAL INFORMATION

Nearest Mainline Station: Stowmarket
Nearest Bus Station: Ipswich
Car Parking: Available on site
Coach Parking: Available on site
Souvenir Shop(s): Yes
Food & Drinks: Yes

SPECIAL INFORMATION

The Mid-Suffolk Light Railway served the heart of the county for 50 years, despite being bankrupt before the first train ran. In a beautiful rural setting, the Museum seeks to preserve the memory of a unique branch line.

OPERATING INFORMATION

Opening Times: Sundays and Bank Holiday Mondays from 5th May to the end of September and also on Wednesdays in August. Open from 11.00am to 5.00pm. Special events open at different times.
Steam Working: 2013 dates: 5th, 6th, 26th & 27th May; 16th June; 7th & 21st July; 4th, 11th, 18th & 25th August; 28th & 29th September; Santa Specials operate on Sundays in December and on New Year's Day. Please contact the railway or check the web site for further information.
Prices: Adult £6.00   Child £3.00
                    Family Ticket £15.00
Tickets allow unlimited travel on the day of issue and act as season tickets for the calendar year (subject to conditions).

Detailed Directions by Car:
The Museum is situated 14 miles north of Ipswich and 28 miles south of Norwich, just off the A140. Look for Mendlesham TV mast and then follow the brown tourist signs from the A140.

MIDLAND RAILWAY – BUTTERLEY

Address: Butterley Station, Ripley, Derbyshire DE5 3QZ
Telephone Nº: (01773) 747674
Year Formed: 1969
Location of Line: Butterley, near Ripley
Length of Line: Standard gauge 3½ miles, Narrow gauge 0.8 mile

Nº of Steam Locos: 23 (+25 Other Locos)
Nº of Members: 2,000
Annual Membership Fee: £19.00
Approx Nº of Visitors P.A.: 130,000
Gauge: Standard, various Narrow gauges and miniature
Web: www.midlandrailway-butterley.co.uk

GENERAL INFORMATION

Nearest Mainline Station: Alfreton (6 miles)
Nearest Bus Station: Bus stop outside Butterley Station.
Car Parking: Free parking at site – ample space
Coach Parking: Free parking at site
Souvenir Shop(s): Yes – at Butterley and Swanwick
Food & Drinks: Yes – both sites + bar on train

SPECIAL INFORMATION

The Centre is a unique project with a huge Museum development together with narrow gauge, miniature & model railways as well as a country park and farm park. Includes an Award-winning Victorian Railwayman's church and Princess Royal Class Locomotive Trust Depot.

OPERATING INFORMATION

Opening Times: Site is open daily throughout the year (except on Christmas Day and Boxing Day). Trains run daily during Easter, all School Holidays and from 24th July to 1st September. Also on most weekends throughout the year and for Santa Specials on other dates in November and December.
Steam Working: Weekends and bank holidays throughout the year and most days in the school holidays. Please phone for further details.
Prices: Adults £13.95   Children £7.00
Senior Citizens £12.95
Family £37.50 (2 adults + 3 children)

Detailed Directions by Car:
From All Parts: From the M1 exit at Junction 28 and take the A38 towards Derby. The Centre is signposted at the junction with the B6179.

NATIONAL RAILWAY MUSEUM – YORK

Address: National Railway Museum,
Leeman Road, York YO26 4XJ
Telephone Nº: 08448 153139
Year Formed: 1975
Location of Line: York
Length of Line: Short demonstration line

Nº of Steam Locos: 79
Nº of Other Locos: 37
Approx Nº of Visitors P.A.: 900,000
Web site: www.nrm.org.uk

GENERAL INFORMATION

Nearest Mainline Station: York (¼ mile)
Nearest Bus Station: York (¼ mile)
Car Parking: On site long stay car park
Coach Parking: On site – free to pre-booked groups
Souvenir Shop(s): Yes
Food & Drinks: Yes

SPECIAL INFORMATION

The Museum is the largest of its kind in the world, housing the Nation's collection of locomotives, carriages, uniforms, posters and an extensive photographic archive. Special events and exhibitions run throughout the year. The Museum is the home of the Mallard – the fastest steam locomotive in the world and Shinkansen, the only Bullet train outside of Japan.

OPERATING INFORMATION

Opening Times: Open daily 10.00am to 6.00pm (closed on 24th, 25th and 26th of December)
Steam Working: School holidays – please phone to confirm details
Prices: Free admission for all
(Excludes some Special events and Steam rides)
Please phone 08448 153139 for further details.

Detailed Directions by Car:
The Museum is located in the centre of York, just behind the Railway Station. It is clearly signposted from all approaches to York.

NENE VALLEY RAILWAY

Address: Wansford Station, Stibbington, Peterborough   PE8 6LR
Telephone Nº: (01780) 784444 enquiries; (01780) 784404 talking timetable
E-mail: nvrorg@nvr.org.uk
Year Formed: 1977
Location: Off A1 to west of Peterborough
Length of Line: 7½ miles

Nº of Steam Locos: 16
Nº of Other Locos: 14
Nº of Members: 1,300
Annual Membership Fee: Adult £14.00; Child £7.00; Senior £11.00; Family £34.00
Approx Nº of Visitors P.A.: 65,000
Gauge: Standard
Web site: www.nvr.org.uk

GENERAL INFORMATION

Nearest Mainline Station: Peterborough (¾ mile)
Nearest Bus Station: Peterborough (Queensgate – ¾ mile)
Car Parking: Free parking at Wansford & Orton Mere
Coach Parking: Free coach parking at Wansford
Souvenir Shop(s): Yes
Food & Drinks: Yes

SPECIAL INFORMATION

The railway is truly international in flavour with British and Continental locomotives and rolling stock.

OPERATING INFORMATION

Opening Times: 2013 dates: Most weekends and Bank Holidays from March to 3rd November. Also open on most Wednesdays from April to the end of September and at various other times. Santa Specials run in December. Please contact the Railway for further details. Trains run from 10.00am to as late as 5.00pm, depending on the time of the year.
Steam Working: Most services are steam hauled apart from on diesel days and times of high fire risk.
Prices: Adult £15.00
Child £8.00
Family £38.00 (2 adults + 3 children)
Senior Citizens/Disabled £12.00

Detailed Directions by Car:
The railway is situated off the southbound carriageway of the A1 between the A47 and A605 junctions – west of Peterborough and south of Stamford.

NORTH NORFOLK RAILWAY (THE POPPY LINE)

Address: Sheringham Station, Sheringham, Norfolk NR26 8RA
Telephone Nº: (01263) 820800
E-mail: enquiries@nnrailway.co.uk
Year Formed: 1975
Location of Line: Sheringham to Holt via Weybourne
Length of Line: 5½ miles

Nº of Steam Locos: 5 (+ visiting locos)
Nº of Other Locos: 4
Nº of Members: 1,800 (M&GNRS)
Annual Membership Fee: £19.00 (Midland & Great Northern Railway Society)
Approx Nº of Visitors P.A.: 150,000
Gauge: Standard
Web site: www.nnrailway.co.uk

Photograph courtesy of Ben Boggis

GENERAL INFORMATION

Nearest Mainline Station: Sheringham (200 yards)
Nearest Bus Station: Outside the Station
Car Parking: Adjacent to Sheringham and Holt
Coach Parking: Adjacent to Sheringham and Holt
Souvenir Shop(s): At Sheringham Station
Food & Drinks: Yes – main catering facilities at Sheringham Station. Light refreshments elsewhere.

SPECIAL INFORMATION

Lunch and evening dinner trains are scheduled throughout the year. Please check the website for times and fares. Weybourne Station is licensed for weddings.

OPERATING INFORMATION

Opening Times: 2013 dates: Daily from Easter to 3rd November plus weekends in March and Santa Specials in December. Special Events: Vintage Transport Festival on 6th & 7th July; Beer Festival 19th to 21st July; Grand Steam Gala 30th August to 1st September; Famous '40s Weekend 21st & 22nd September. Please contact the railway for information about further Special Event dates.
Steam Working: 9.45am to 4.30pm (high season)
Prices: Adult £11.00
Child £7.50 (Under 5s free of charge)
Family £37.00 (2 adults + 2 children)
Senior Citizens £10.00
Dogs and Bicycles £1.00 each
The prices shown above are for all-day hop-on, hop-off, Day Rover tickets.

Detailed Directions by Car:
Sheringham Station is situated just off the A149. Holt Station is located at High Kelling, just off the A148.

NORTH TYNESIDE STEAM RAILWAY

Address: Stephenson Railway Museum, Middle Engine Lane, North Shields, NE29 8DX	**N° of Steam Locos**: 5
	N° of Other Locos: 3
	N° of Members: 30
Telephone N°: (0191) 200-7146	**Annual Membership Fee**: £9.00
Year Formed: 1986	**Approx N° of Visitors P.A.**: 30,000
Location: Stephenson Railway Museum	**Gauge**: Standard
Length of Line: 1½ miles	**Web site**: www.ntsra.org.uk

GENERAL INFORMATION

Nearest Mainline Station: Newcastle Central (5 miles) or for the Metro Percy Main (1½ miles)
Nearest Bus Station: North Shields
Car Parking: Free parking available on site
Coach Parking: Free parking available on site
Souvenir Shop(s): Yes
Food & Drinks: Hot drinks machine available

SPECIAL INFORMATION

A programme of events and activities is available from the Museum on request. Use the following URL:

www.twmuseums.org.uk/stephenson

OPERATING INFORMATION

Opening Times: 2013 dates: Daily from 29th March to 3rd November and daily during School Holidays, 11.00am to 4.00pm. Santa Specials operate every weekend from 30th November to 22nd December.
Steam Working: Sundays and Bank Holiday Mondays from June to September.
Prices: Adult Return £2.45
Child Return £1.20
Family Return £6.10
Note: Admission to the museum is free of charge.

Detailed Directions by Car:
The Railway is adjacent to the Silverlink Retail Park approximately ½ mile from the junction between the A19 and A1058. From the A19/A1058 junction look for the signs for 'Silverlink' before following the Brown tourist signs to the Stephenson Railway Museum.

NORTH YORKSHIRE MOORS RAILWAY

Address: Pickering Station, Pickering, North Yorkshire YO18 7AJ **Telephone Nº**: (01751) 472508 (enquiries) **Year Formed**: 1967 **Location of Line**: Pickering to Grosmont via stations at Levisham and Goathland **Length of Line**: 18 miles **Nº of Steam Locos**: 20	**Nº of Other Locos**: 12 **Nº of Members**: 8,000 **Annual Membership Fee**: Adult £18.00; Over 60s £14.00 **Approx Nº of Visitors P.A.**: 330,000 **Gauge**: Standard **Web site**: www.nymr.co.uk **E-mail**: info@nymr.co.uk

GENERAL INFORMATION

Nearest Mainline Station: Grosmont (adjacent to the NYMR station) or Whitby
Nearest Bus Station: Pickering (½ mile)
Car Parking: Available at each station
Coach Parking: Available at Pickering & Grosmont
Souvenir Shop(s): Yes – at Pickering, Goathland, and Grosmont Stations plus Grosmont MPD
Food & Drinks: Pickering, Grosmont & Goathland

SPECIAL INFORMATION

The NYMR runs through the spectacular North York Moors National Park and is the most popular steam railway in the country. As seen in 'Heartbeat' and the first Harry Potter film. The railway now operates extended services to and from Whitby.

OPERATING INFORMATION

Opening Times: 2013 dates: Open on weekends in March then daily from 23rd March to 3rd November plus Santa Specials in December. Please contact the railway for further information.
Steam Working: Usually daily – please phone the Railway for timetable information
Prices: Adult Day Rover £18.00 – £24.00
Child Day Rover £9.00 – £12.00
Senior Citizen Day Rover £16.00 – £21.00
Family Day Rover Tickets £36.00 – £48.00
(2 adults and up to 4 children)
Note: The higher fares are for trips through to Whitby.

Detailed Directions by Car:
From the South: Follow the A64 past York to the Malton bypass then take the A169 to Pickering; From the North: Take A171 towards Whitby then follow the minor road through Egton to Grosmont.

NORTHAMPTON & LAMPORT RAILWAY

Address: Pitsford & Bramford Station, Pitsford Road, Chapel Brampton, Northampton NN6 8BA **Telephone N°**: (01604) 820327 (infoline) **Year Formed**: 1983 (became operational in November 1995) **Length of Line**: 1½ miles at present	**N° of Steam Locos**: 6 **N° Other Locos**: 6 **N° of Members**: 350 **Annual Membership Fee**: Adult £12.00 and Senior Citizen £6.00 **Approx N° of Visitors P.A.**: 9,300 **Gauge**: Standard **Web site**: www.nlr.org.uk

GENERAL INFORMATION

Nearest Mainline Station: Northampton (5 miles)
Nearest Bus Station: Northampton (5 miles)
Car Parking: Free parking at site
Coach Parking: Free parking at site
Souvenir Shop(s): Yes
Food & Drinks: Yes

SPECIAL INFORMATION

The railway operates on a section of the old London & North Western Railway line between Northampton and Market Harborough and became operational again on 18th November 1995. Work is currently underway on a southern extension to the line and the N&LR hope to open this in 2013.

OPERATING INFORMATION

Opening Times: 2013 dates: Sundays and Bank holidays from 3rd March until 27th October and Santa Specials in December. Open from 10.30am to 4.30pm (the last train runs at 3.30pm). Please contact the railway for a more detailed timetable.
Steam Working: Bank Holiday weekends and Santa Specials in December. Steam and Diesel trains run on alternating Sundays during other times. Please contact the railway for further information.
Prices: Adult £4.80
Child £3.80 (Under-2s ride free)
Family £15.50 (2 adults + 2 children)
Senior Citizen £3.80
Fares may vary on Special Event days.

Detailed Directions by Car:
The station is situated along the Pitsford road at Chapel Brampton, approximately 5 miles north of Northampton. Heading north out of town, it is signposted to the right on the A5199 (A50) Welford Road at Chapel Brampton crossroads or on the left on the A508 Market Harborough road at the Pitsford turn.

NORTHANTS. IRONSTONE RAILWAY TRUST

Address: Hunsbury Hill Museum, Hunsbury Hill Country Park, West Hunsbury, Northampton NN4 9UW **Telephone Nº:** (01604) 702031 **Year Formed:** 1974 **Location of Line:** Hunsbury Hill Country Park, Northampton **Length of Line:** Two-thirds of a mile	**Nº of Steam Locos:** 3 **Nº of Other Locos:** 4 **Nº of Members:** Approximately 60 **Annual Membership Fee:** £10.00 Adult **Approx Nº of Visitors P.A.:** Not known **Gauge:** Standard **Web site:** www.nirt.co.uk

GENERAL INFORMATION

Nearest Mainline Station: Northampton (2½ miles)
Nearest Bus Station: Northampton (3 miles)
Car Parking: Large free car park at the site
Coach Parking: Available at the site on request
Souvenir Shop(s): Yes
Food & Drinks: Yes

SPECIAL INFORMATION

The Railway has recently re-opened after a major rebuild and now operates along two-thirds of a mile of track. The Museum is dedicated to the Ironstone industry of Northamptonshire.

OPERATING INFORMATION

Opening Times: The museum is open during Easter weekend, Spring Bank Holiday weekend then the first Sunday of the month from June to October and also on other Bank Holidays throughout the year. Trains run at these times also. There may also be a number of special events throughout the year (including Santa Specials) – please contact the railway for further information.
Steam Working: An hourly service runs between 11.00am and 5.00pm.
Prices: Adult £3.00 Child £2.00
Concessions £1.50
Admission to the museum and site is free of charge but donations are always welcome.

Detailed Directions by Car:
Exit the M1 at Junction 15A, and follow the road for approximately ½ mile. Turn left onto the A43 and after approximately 1 mile take the 3rd exit at the roundabout onto Danes Camp Way (A45). After ½ mile take the 4th exit at the roundabout onto Hunsbury Hill Road. Continue over two mini-roundabouts past the Rose & Claret Public House. The entrance to Hunsbury Hill Country Park for the railway is on the left.

PEAK RAIL PLC

Address: Matlock Station, Matlock, Derbyshire DE4 3NA
Telephone N°: (01629) 580381
Fax N°: (01629) 760645
Year Formed: 1975
Location: Matlock to Rowsley South
Length of Line: Approximately 4½ miles

N° of Steam Locos: 4 **Other Locos:** 20+
N° of Members: 1,700
Annual Adult Membership Fee: £16.00
Approx N° of Visitors P.A.: 70,000
Gauge: Standard
Web site: www.peakrail.co.uk
E-mail: peakrail@peakrail.co.uk

GENERAL INFO

Nearest Mainline Station: Matlock
Nearest Bus Station: Matlock
Car Parking: Paid car parking at Matlock Station. 200 free parking spaces available at Rowsley South Station and 20 free spaces at Darley Dale Station
Coach Parking: Free parking at Rowsley South
Souvenir Shop(s): Yes
Food & Drinks: Yes – R.M.B. Buffet on the train and the Rowsley Buffet at Rowsley South Station.

SPECIAL INFO

The Palatine Restaurant Car is available whilst travelling on the train and caters for Sunday Lunches, Teas and Party Bookings. Coach parties are welcomed when the railway is operating.

OPERATING INFO

Opening Times: Weekends and Bank Holidays throughout most of the year. Also Tuesdays from April to September, Wednesdays from May to September and some other dates including most Thursdays in August. Santa Specials run during weekends in December. Please contact the railway for further information. Trains run from 11.15am to 4.20pm.
Steam Working: All services throughout the year.
Prices: Adult Return £7.50
        Children – Under-3s Free
        Children – Ages 3-5 £2.00
        Children – Ages 6-15 £4.00
        Senior Citizen Return £6.00
        Family Ticket £23.00
        (2 adults + 3 children)

Detailed Directions by Car:
Exit the M1 at Junctions 28, 29 or 30 and follow signs towards Matlock. From North and South take A6 direct to Matlock. From Stoke-on-Trent, take the A52 to Ashbourne, then the A5035 to Matlock. Upon reaching Matlock follow the brown tourist signs.

PLYM VALLEY RAILWAY

Address: Marsh Mills Station, Coypool Road, Plympton, Plymouth   PL7 4NW
Telephone Nº: (01752) 330881
Year Formed: 1980
Location of Line: Marsh Mills to Plym Bridge Platform
Length of Line: 1¼ mile

Nº of Steam Locos: 4
Nº of Other Locos: 4
Nº of Members: 250
Annual Membership Fee: £12.00
Approx Nº of Visitors P.A.: 5,000
Gauge: Standard
Web site: www.plymrail.co.uk

GENERAL INFORMATION

Nearest Mainline Station: Plymouth (4 miles)
Nearest Bus Station: Plymouth (3 miles)
Car Parking: Available on site
Coach Parking: Available on site
Souvenir Shop(s): Yes
Food & Drinks: Light snacks available

SPECIAL INFORMATION

2012 saw the opening of the extension of the line to Plym Bridge. This is a section of the former Great Western branch line which from Tavistock Junction through to Launceston. The railway now plans to further develop their visitor facilities at Marsh Mills.

OPERATING INFORMATION

Opening Times: Open for static viewing on most Sundays from 11.00am to 5.00pm. 2013 operating dates: 14th & 28th July; 11th, 24th & 25th August; 8th & 22nd September; 27th October and Santa Specials on 1st, 8th, 15th & 22nd December. Trains run between 1.00pm to 4.00pm on all of these dates. Please contact the railway for details of any further operating dates.
Steam Working: Most operating days. Please contact the railway for further details.
Prices: Adult Return £4.00
               Child Return £2.00
Note: There is no charge to visit the station.

Detailed Directions by Car:
Leave the A38 at the Marsh Mills turn-off and take the B3416 towards Plympton. Turn left into Coypool Road just after the McDonalds restaurant. From Plymouth City Centre, take the A374 to Marsh Mills, then as above.

PONTYPOOL & BLAENAVON RAILWAY

Address: 13a Broad Street, Blaenavon, Torfaen NP4 9ND	**Nᵒ of Steam Locos**: 6
e-mail: info@pbrly.co.uk	**Nᵒ of Other Locos**: 5 + 4 DMUs
Telephone Nᵒ: (01495) 792263	**Nᵒ of Members**: 350
Year Formed: 1980 (Opened 1983)	**Annual Membership Fee**: £14.00
Location of Line: Just off the B4248 between Blaenavon and Brynmawr	**Approx Nᵒ of Visitors P.A.**: 12,700
Length of Line: 2 miles	**Gauge**: Standard
	Web site: www.pontypool-and-blaenavon.co.uk

GENERAL INFORMATION

Nearest Mainline Station: Abergavenny (5 miles)
Nearest Bus Station: Blaenavon Town (1½ miles) – regular bus service within ¼ mile (except Sundays)
Car Parking: Free parking for 50 cars on site
Coach Parking: Available on site
Souvenir Shop(s): Yes – at the Station and also a shop at 13 Broad Street, Blaenavon
Food & Drinks: Light refreshments on the train and at the station.

SPECIAL INFORMATION

The railway operates over very steep gradients, is run entirely by volunteers and is the highest standard gauge preserved railway in England and Wales.

OPERATING INFORMATION

Opening Times: 2013 dates: Every weekend and Bank Holiday Monday from 29th March to 15th September. Also the fourth weekend of October, Wednesdays in August and Santa Specials on weekends in December. Please phone the Railway for details or check the web site for other dates.
Steam Working: Trains are steam-hauled during Peak days and special steam days. Diesel locos or DMUs may be used on quiet days. Please contact the Railway for further information.
Prices: Adult Return £6.00
Child Return £3.50
Family Return £15.50 (2 adult + 3 children)
Fares and conditions may vary for Special Events.

Detailed Directions by Car:
From All Parts: The railway is situated just off the B4248 between Blaenavon and Brynmawr and is well signposted as you approach Blaenavon. Use Junction 25A if using the M4 from the East, or Junction 26 from the West. Head for Pontypool. From the Midlands use the M50, A40 then A465 to Brynmawr. From North & West Wales consider using the 'Heads of the Valleys' A465 to Brynmawr. As you approach the Railway, look out for the Colliery water tower – you can't miss it!

RIBBLE STEAM RAILWAY

Address: Chain Caul Road, Preston, PR2 2PD **Telephone Nº:** (01772) 728800 **Year Formed:** 2005 **Location:** West of Preston City Centre **Length of Line:** 3 mile round trip	**Nº of Steam Locos:** 24 **Nº of Other Locos:** 19 **Nº of Members:** 400 **Annual Membership Fee:** £15.00 **Approx Nº of Visitors P.A.:** 20,000+ **Gauge:** Standard **Web site:** www.ribblesteam.org.uk

GENERAL INFORMATION

Nearest Mainline Station: Preston (2 miles)
Nearest Bus Station: Preston (2 miles)
Car Parking: Available on site
Coach Parking: Available on site
Souvenir Shop(s): Yes
Food & Drinks: Available

SPECIAL INFORMATION

The line traverses a swing bridge across the Marina entrance – the only preserved steam line in Britain to have such a feature! The railway also has the largest collection of standard gauge industrial locomotives housed under cover in the UK.

OPERATING INFORMATION

Opening Times: 2013 dates: Open 10.30am to 5.00pm on Sundays in April then weekends and Bank Holidays from May to 6th October. Also open on Wednesdays in August and for Santa specials on weekends in December. Please contact the railway for details of further operating days.
Steam Working: On all days when the railway is open to the public. Trains run hourly from 11.00am to 4.00pm.
Prices: Adult Return £6.00
Child/Concessionary Return £4.00
Family Return £18.00
Note: Prices may differ to those shown above.

Detailed Directions by Car:
From All Parts: The Railway is located on the Riversway/Docklands Business and Residential Park, just off the A583 Lytham/Blackpool road and approximately 1½ miles to the west of Preston City Centre. Follow the Brown Tourist signs from the A583 for the railway.

ROYAL DEESIDE RAILWAY

Address: Milton of Crathes, Crathes, Banchory AB31 5QH
Telephone Nº: (01330) 844416
E-mail: info@deeside-railway.co.uk
Year Formed: 1996
Location of Line: Milton of Crathes
Length of Line: 1 mile

Nº of Steam Locos: 1 (may leave in 2013)
Nº of Other Locos: 2
Nº of Members: 250
Annual Membership Fee: £15.00
Approx Nº of Visitors P.A.: 3,000
Gauge: Standard
Web site: www.deeside-railway.co.uk

GENERAL INFORMATION

Nearest Mainline Station: Aberdeen (14 miles)
Nearest Bus Station: Stagecoach Bluebird bus stop nearby on A93.
Car Parking: Free parking available on site
Coach Parking: Free parking available on site
Souvenir Shop(s): Yes – inside a static carriage
Food & Drinks: Yes – inside a static carriage

SPECIAL INFORMATION

The line is gradually being extended to Banchary and, when completed, will be 2 miles in length.

OPERATING INFORMATION

Opening Times: 2013 dates: Weekends from April to September and Wednesdays in July and early August plus some other dates. Also open for Santa Specials each weekend in December. Please contact the railway for further details.
Steam Working: 2013 dates were not agreed at the time of going to press. Please contact the railway for details of steaming dates.
Prices: Adults £4.00 (£6.00 Steam days)
　　　　　 Children £2.00 (£3.00 Steam days)
　　　　　 Senior Citizens £2.50 (£4.00 Steam days)

Detailed Directions by Car:
From the South: Take the A90 to Stonehaven. Exit onto the B979 for Stonehaven and follow into the town square. Turn left at the traffic lights and follow signs for the A957 to Banchory (Historic Slug Road). Follow this road for 14 mile via Durris to Crathes and the junction with the A93. Turn left and follow the Brown Tourist signs, turning left for the railway after approximately 600 yards; From the North & West: Follow the A980 to Banchory and turn left onto the A93. Turn right following the Brown Tourist signs for the railway.

RUSHDEN TRANSPORT MUSEUM

Address: Rushden Station,
Station Approach, Rushden, NN10 0AW
Telephone Nº: (01933) 318988
Year Formed: 1985
Location of Line: Rushden, Northants.
Length of Line: ½ mile (each paid trip is 2½ miles in distance)

Nº of Steam Locos: 3
Nº of Other Locos: 4
Nº of Members: Approximately 600
Annual Membership Fee: £18.00 (Family)
Approx Nº of Visitors P.A.: 5,000
Gauge: Standard
Web site: www.rhts.co.uk

GENERAL INFORMATION

Nearest Mainline Station: Wellingborough (5 miles)
Nearest Bus Station: Northampton (14 miles)
Car Parking: Available on site. On operating days a nearby public car park must be used.
Coach Parking: None
Souvenir Shop(s): Yes
Food & Drinks: Available on operating weekends

SPECIAL INFORMATION

The Rushden Transport Museum is situated in the old Midland Railway Station of 1894 which once formed part of the Wellingborough to Higham Ferrers branch line. Taken over by the Rushden Historical Transport Society in 1984 the station also provides the society with a social club.

OPERATING INFORMATION

Opening Times: The Museum is open from Easter until the end of October on Saturdays (2.00pm to 4.00pm) and Sundays (10.00am to 4.00pm)
A wide variety of special events are scheduled for 2013. For further details, either check the museum's web site or phone for information.
Steam Working: Please contact the museum for further information.
Prices: Admission to the museum is usually free but charges will be made on Special Event days.

Detailed Directions by Car:
From All Parts: Take the A6 to the Rushden Bypass (to the south of the A45) and turn into John Clark Way by the large grey warehouses. The Station is located on the right-hand side of the road after approximately 400 yards.

RUTLAND RAILWAY MUSEUM

Address: Cottesmore Iron Ore Mines Siding, Ashwell Road, Cottesmore, Oakham, Rutland   LE15 7BX
Telephone Nº: (01572) 813203
Year Formed: 1979
Location of Line: Between the villages of Cottesmore and Ashwell
Length of Line: ¾ mile

Nº of Steam Locos: 13
Nº of Other Locos: 13
Nº of Members: 275
Annual Membership Fee: £10.00
Approx Nº of Visitors P.A.: 8,000
Gauge: Standard
Web site: www.rocks-by-rail.org

GENERAL INFORMATION

Nearest Mainline Station: Oakham (4 miles)
Nearest Bus Station: Cottesmore/Ashwell (1½ miles)
Car Parking: Available at the site
Coach Parking: Limited space available
Souvenir Shop(s): On open days
Food & Drinks: On open days

SPECIAL INFORMATION

This Industrial Railway Heritage centre is located at the end of the former Ashwell-Cottesmore mineral branch and is based at the former exchange sidings. Major structural work is taking place and it is hoped that passenger services will resume during 2013.

OPERATING INFORMATION

Opening Times: Static viewing on Sundays from 11.00am to 4.00pm plus Tuesday and Thursday afternoons throughout the year.
Steam Working: Please contact the museum for further information.
Prices: Admission to the museum is free of charge (though donations are gratefully received). Charges will be made on Steam operating days and for other Special Events. However, no dates had been confirmed for 2013 at the time of going to press. Please contact the museum for further information.

Detailed Directions by Car:
From All Parts: The Museum is situated 4 miles north of Oakham between Ashwell and Cottesmore. Follow the brown tourist signs from the B668 Oakham to A1 road or the signs from the A606 Stamford to Oakham Road.

SCOTTISH INDUSTRIAL RAILWAY CENTRE

Address: Dunaskin Open Air Museum, Waterside, Patna, Ayrshire   KA6 7JF
Telephone Nº: (01292) 313579 (Evenings & Weekends)
Year Formed: 1974
Location of Line: Dunaskin Ironworks
Length of Line: A third of a mile

Nº of Steam Locos: 9
Nº of Other Locos: 15
Nº of Members: 180
Annual Membership Fee: £12.50
Approx Nº of Visitors P.A.: 3,500
Gauge: Standard
Web site: www.arpg.org.uk

GENERAL INFORMATION

Nearest Mainline Station: Ayr (10 miles)
Nearest Bus Station: ½ hourly bus service from Ayr – phone (01292) 613500 for more information
Car Parking: Free parking available at the site
Coach Parking: Free parking available at the site
Souvenir Shop(s): Yes
Food & Drinks: Soft drinks and confectionery only

SPECIAL INFORMATION

The Railway is operated by the Ayrshire Railway Preservation Group and is located at the former Dunaskin Heritage Centre which was unfortunately forced to close in 2006.

OPERATING INFORMATION

Opening Times: 2013 operating dates: 26th May; 23rd & 30th June; 7th, 14th, 21st & 28th July; 4th, 11th, 18th & 25th August; 1st and 22nd September. Open from 11.00am to 4.30pm on these days (last admission at 4.00pm). Please contact the railway or check the web site for further details.
Steam Working: On all operating dates.
Prices: Adults £5.00
  Children £3.00 (Free for ages 3 and under)
  Senior Citizens £3.00
  Family Ticket £13.00 (2 adults + 3 children)

Detailed Directions by Car:
From All Parts: Dunaskin Open Air Museum is located adjacent to the A713 Ayr to Castle Douglas road approximately 10 miles to the southwest of Ayr.

SEVERN VALLEY RAILWAY

Address: Railway Station, Bewdley,
Worcestershire   DY12 1BG
Telephone Nº: (01299) 403816
Year Formed: 1965
Location of Line: Kidderminster
(Worcs.) to Bridgnorth (Shropshire)
Length of Line: 16 miles

Nº of Steam Locos: 27
Nº of Other Locos: 12
Nº of Members: 13,000
Annual Membership Fee: Adult £18.00
Approx Nº of Passengers P.A.: 248,000
Gauge: Standard
Web site: www.svr.co.uk

GENERAL INFORMATION

Nearest Mainline Station: Kidderminster (adjacent)
Nearest Bus Station: Kidderminster (500 yards)
Car Parking: Large car park at Kidderminster.
Spaces also available at other stations.
Coach Parking: At Kidderminster
Souvenir Shop(s): At Kidderminster & Bridgnorth
Food & Drinks: On most trains. Also at Bewdley,
Bridgnorth, Kidderminster and The Engine House

SPECIAL INFORMATION

The SVR has numerous special events including an
Autumn Steam Gala, 1940's weekend, Classic Car &
Bike Day and visits by Santa! 'The Engine House', the
railway's visitor and education centre, is a further
attraction at Highley.

OPERATING INFORMATION

Opening Times: 2013 dates: Weekends throughout
the year. Also daily from 4th May to 6th October and
during local School Holidays. Santa Specials run at
weekends and on some other dates in December.
Please contact the railway for further details.
Steam Working: Train times vary depending on
timetable information. Phone for details.
Prices: Adult Day Rover £17.00
             Child Day Rover £11.00
             Senior Citizen Day Rover £15.50
Note: Entrance to The Engine House is included in
the above prices and upgrades to First Class travel
are also available. Discounts are available for
advance bookings.

Detailed Directions by Car:
For Kidderminster take M5 and exit Junction 3 or Junction 6. Follow the brown tourist signs for the railway;
From the South: Take the M40 then M42 to Junction 1 for the A448 from Bromsgrove to Kidderminster.

SNIBSTON COLLIERY RAILWAY

Address: Ashby Road, Coalville, LE67 3LN
Telephone Nº: (01530) 278444
Year Formed: 2001
Location of Line: Snibston Colliery
Length of Line: 1,100 yards

Nº of Steam Locos: 4
Nº of Other Locos: 2
Approx Nº of Visitors P.A.: 100,000
Gauge: Standard
Web site: www.snibston.com

GENERAL INFORMATION

Nearest Mainline Station: Loughborough (10 miles)
Nearest Bus Station: Loughborough (10 miles)
Car Parking: Available on site
Coach Parking: Available on site
Souvenir Shop(s): Yes
Food & Drinks: Available

SPECIAL INFORMATION

The Railway is located on the site of the former Snibston Colliery which also hosts an interactive museum, outside play areas, a Country Park and a nature reserve.

OPERATING INFORMATION

Opening Times: From November to March open on weekdays, 10.00am to 3.00pm and on weekends from 10.00am to 5.00pm. From April to October, Snibston is open daily from 10.00am to 5.00pm. Trains operate only on certain dates. Please contact the Museum for further information.
Steam Working: No usual steam operation. Please contact the Museum for further details.
Prices: Adults £7.95 (Train rides £1.70 extra)
 Children £5.50 (Trains rides £1.10 extra)
 Concessions £6.25 (Train rides £1.50 extra)
 Family £24.25 (2+2) or £29.00 (2 + 3)
 (Train rides £4.50 extra)

Detailed Directions by Car:
From All Parts: Exit the A42 at the A511 (Coalville) exit and follow the signs for Snibston.

SOMERSET & DORSET RAILWAY TRUST MUSEUM

Address: The Railway Station, Washford, Somerset   TA23 0PP
Telephone Nº: (01984) 640869
Year Formed: 1966
Location of Line: Washford Station
Length of Line: Station sidings only

Nº of Steam Locos: 2
Nº of Other Locos: 1
Nº of Members: –
Annual Membership Fee: £18.00 (Adult)
Approx Nº of Visitors P.A.: 3,000
Gauge: Standard
Web site: www.sdrt.org.uk

GENERAL INFORMATION

Nearest Mainline Station: Taunton (17 miles)
Nearest Bus Station: Taunton (17 miles)
Car Parking: Available on site
Coach Parking: None
Souvenir Shop(s): Yes
Food & Drinks: None

SPECIAL INFORMATION

The Museum of the Somerset & Dorset Railway Trust contains a mass of exhibits about and memorabilia of this much loved line. This includes a reconstruction of Midford signal box and carriages and wagons including some undergoing restoration.

OPERATING INFORMATION

Opening Times: A full list of opening dates had not been set at the time of going to press. Please check the Museum's web site or phone for further details.
Steam Working: Please contact the Museum or check the web site for further details.
Prices: Please contact the Museum for further information.

Detailed Directions by Car:
The Museum is located at the Railway Station in Washford Village on the A39 Bridgwater to Minehead road.

SOUTH DEVON RAILWAY

<table>
<tr><td>

Address: Buckfastleigh Station,
Buckfastleigh, Devon   TQ11 0DZ
Telephone Nº: 0843 357-1420
Year Formed: 1969
Location of Line: Totnes to Buckfastleigh
via Staverton
Length of Line: 7 miles

</td><td>

Nº of Steam Locos: 13
Nº of Other Locos: 11
Nº of Members: 3,500
Annual Membership Fee: £17.00
Approx Nº of Visitors P.A.: 100,000+
Gauge: Standard
Web Site: www.southdevonrailway.co.uk

</td></tr>
</table>

GENERAL INFORMATION

Nearest Mainline Station: Totnes (¼ mile)
Nearest Bus Station: Totnes (½ mile), Buckfastleigh
(Station Road)
Car Parking: Free parking at Buckfastleigh,
Council/NR parking at Totnes
Coach Parking: As above
Souvenir Shop(s): Yes – at Buckfastleigh
Food & Drinks: Yes – at Buckfastleigh & on train

SPECIAL INFORMATION

The railway was opened in 1872 as the Totnes,
Buckfastleigh & Ashburton Railway.

OPERATING INFORMATION

Opening Times: 2013 dates: Daily from 16th
March to 3rd November. Santa Specials also run in
December. Please contact the railway for further
details.
Steam Working: Almost all trains are steam hauled.
Prices: Adult Return £12.00   Child Return £7.00
            Family Return £34.60
                (2 adults + 2 children)
            Senior Citizen Return £11.00
Note: Extra discounts are available for large groups.

E-mail: trains@southdevonrailway.org

Detailed Directions by Car:
Buckfastleigh is half way between Exeter and Plymouth on the A38 Devon Expressway. Totnes can be reached by
taking the A385 from Paignton and Torquay. Brown tourist signs give directions for the railway.

SPA VALLEY RAILWAY

Address: West Station, Tunbridge Wells, Kent TN2 5QY	**Nº of Steam Locos**: 9
Telephone Nº: (01892) 537715	**Nº of Other Locos**: 7
Year Formed: 1985	**Nº of Members**: Approximately 850
Location of Line: Tunbridge Wells West to Groombridge and Eridge	**Annual Membership Fee**: £20.00
	Approx Nº of Visitors P.A.: 36,000
Length: 5 miles	**Gauge**: Standard
	Web Site: www.spavalleyrailway.co.uk

GENERAL INFORMATION

Nearest Mainline Station: Eridge (cross-platform interchange with the mainline)
Nearest Bus Stop: Outside Sainsbury's (100yds)
Car Parking: Available in Tunbridge Wells nearby in Major Yorks Road, Union House & Linden Close
Coach Parking: Montacute Road (150 yards)
Souvenir Shop(s): Yes   **Food & Drinks**: Yes

SPECIAL INFORMATION

The Railway's Tunbridge Wells Terminus is in a historic and unique L.B. & S.C.R. engine shed. The extension to Eridge is now open at weekends and on public holidays and tickets inclusive of entry to Groombridge Place Gardens are also available.

OPERATING INFORMATION

Opening Times: 2013 dates: Weekends and Bank Holidays from 2nd March to 3rd November. Some weekdays during School Holidays and also Santa Specials during on weekends during December.
Steam Working: Most services are steam-hauled. Trains run from 10.15am to 5.30pm (10.50am to 3.30pm midweek and during low season).
Prices: Adult Return £10.00   Child Return £5.00
         Senior Citizen Return £9.00
         Family Return £26.00 (2 adult + 2 child)
Discounts are available for groups of 20 or more.
Fares vary on some special event days.
Fares allow unlimited travel on the day of issue except for special event days.

Detailed Directions by Car:
The Spa Valley Railway is in the southern part of Tunbridge Wells, 100 yards off the A26. Tunbridge Wells Station is adjacent to Sainsbury's and Homebase.   For Eridge Station (Satnav TN3 9LE), follow signs off the A26.

STEAM – MUSEUM OF THE GREAT WESTERN RAILWAY

Address: STEAM – Museum of the Great Western Railway, Firefly Avenue, Swindon SN2 2EY **Telephone Nº**: (01793) 466646 **Year Formed**: 2000	**Nº of Steam Locos**: 6 **Nº of Other Locos**: 1 **Approx Nº of Visitors P.A.**: 100,000 **Web site**: www.steam-museum.org.uk **E-mail**: adminsteam@swindon.gov.uk

GENERAL INFORMATION

Nearest Mainline Station: Swindon (10 min. walk)
Nearest Bus Station: Swindon (10 minute walk)
Car Parking: Ample parking space available in the Outlet Centre (charges apply)
Coach Parking: Free parking on site and nearby
Souvenir Shop(s): Yes
Food & Drinks: There is a Café within the Museum

SPECIAL INFORMATION

STEAM tells the story of the men and women who built the Great Western Railway.

OPERATING INFORMATION

Opening Times: Open daily all year round from 10.00am to 5.00pm (last admission is 4.00pm). Closed from 24th to 26th December and 1st January.
Steam Working: During some special events only – please contact the Museum for details.
Prices: Adult Tickets £6.60
Child Tickets £4.40
Family Tickets £16.10 – £20.80
Senior Citizen Tickets £4.40
Children under 5 are admitted free
Note: Season tickets are also available and prices are correct at the time of going to press.

Detailed Directions by Car:
Exit the M4 at Junction 16 and follow the brown tourist signs to 'Outlet Centre'. Similarly follow the brown signs from all other major routes.   From the Railway Station: STEAM is a 10 to 15 minute walk and is accessible through the pedestrian tunnel – entrance by Emlyn Square.

STRATHSPEY STEAM RAILWAY

Address: Aviemore Station, Dalfaber
Road, Aviemore, Inverness-shire,
PH22 1PY
Telephone Nº: (01479) 810725
Year Formed: 1971
Location of Line: Aviemore to Boat of
Garten and Broomhill, Inverness-shire
Length of Line: 9½ miles at present

Nº of Steam Locos: 7
Nº of Other Locos: 10
Nº of Members: 850
Annual Membership Fee: £21.00
Approx Nº of Visitors P.A.: 56,000
Gauge: Standard
Web site: www.strathspeyrailway.co.uk

GENERAL INFORMATION

Nearest Mainline Station: Aviemore – Strathspey
trains depart from Platform 3
Nearest Bus Station: Aviemore (adjacent)
Car Parking: Available at all stations
Coach Parking: Available at Aviemore and
Broomhill stations
Souvenir Shop(s): Yes – at Aviemore and Boat of
Garten Stations
Food & Drinks: Available on Steam trains only

SPECIAL INFORMATION

The railway featured in the BBC series 'Monarch of
the Glen' and operates from Aviemore Station.

OPERATING INFORMATION

Opening Times: Daily in July and August, most
days in April, May, June. Most days in September
and October (but for Mondays and Tuesdays) and
other dates in December. Please phone for details.
Generally open from 9.30am to 4.30pm.
Steam Working: Most trains are steam-hauled but
diesel power is used where there are fire risks.
Please phone the Railway for details.
Prices: Adult Return £13.00
Child Return £6.50
Family Return £33.00
        (2 adults and up to 3 children)
Senior Citizen Return £11.00

Detailed Directions by Car:
For Aviemore Station from South: Take the A9 then B970 and turn left between the railway & river bridges. For
Boat of Garten from North; Take the A9 then A938 to Carr Bridge, then B9153 and A95 and follow the signs; From
North East: Take A95 to Boat of Garten or Broomhill (3½ miles South from Grantown-on-Spey.

SWANAGE RAILWAY

Address: Station House, Railway Station, Swanage, Dorset BH19 1HB **Telephone Nº:** (01929) 425800 **Year Formed:** 1976 **Location of Line:** Swanage to Norden **Length of Line:** 6 miles **Gauge:** Standard	**Nº of Steam Locos:** 4 **Nº of Other Locos:** 4 **Nº of Members:** 4,200 **Annual Membership Fee:** Adult £21.00; Senior Citizen £15.00; Family £42.00 **Approx Nº of Visitors P.A.:** 200,300 **Web site:** www.swanagerailway.co.uk

GENERAL INFORMATION

Nearest Mainline Station: Wareham (10 miles)
Nearest Bus Station: Swanage Station (adjacent)
Car Parking: Park & Ride at Norden. Public car parks in Swanage (5 minutes walk)
Coach Parking: Available at Norden
Souvenir Shop(s): Yes – at Swanage Station
Food & Drinks: Yes – buffet available on trains and also Swanage Station Buffet and at Norden.

SPECIAL INFORMATION

The railway runs along part of the route of the old Swanage to Wareham railway, opened in 1885.

OPERATING INFORMATION

Opening Times: Weekends from early March then daily from 23rd March to 3rd November. Also open on some other dates throughout the year. Usually open from 9.30am to 5.00pm although trains may run later from May to September and evening services operate during some dates in the summer.
Steam Working: Most services are steam-hauled. Please check with the Railway for further details.
Prices: Adult Return £10.50
Child Return £7.00
Family Ticket £30.00
Note: Prices shown above are the maximum return prices and may be subject to change.

Detailed Directions by Car:
Norden Park & Ride Station is situated off the A351 on the approach to Corfe Castle. Swanage Station is situated in the centre of the town, just a few minutes walk from the beach. Take the A351 to reach Swanage.

SWINDON & CRICKLADE RAILWAY

Address: Blunsdon Station, Tadpole Lane, Blunsdon, Swindon, Wilts SN25 2DA	**Nº of Steam Locos:** 6
	Nº of Other Locos: 8
Phone Nº: (01793) 771615	**Nº of Members:** 700
Year Formed: 1978	**Annual Membership Fee:** £14.00
Location of Line: Blunsdon to Hayes Knoll	**Approx Nº of Visitors P.A.:** 16,000
Length of Line: 2½ miles	**Gauge:** Standard

GENERAL INFORMATION

Nearest Mainline Station: Swindon (5 miles)
Nearest Bus Station: Bus stop at Oakhurst (¾ mile)
Car Parking: Free parking at Blunsdon Station
Coach Parking: Free parking at Blunsdon Station
Souvenir Shop(s): Yes
Food & Drinks: Yes

SPECIAL INFORMATION

The Engine Shed at Hayes Knoll Station is open to the public.

Web site: www.swindon-cricklade-railway.org

OPERATING INFORMATION

Opening Times: The Railway is open every weekend and Bank Holiday from February to December. Santa Specials run in December and other various special events throughout the year also have Steam train rides. Open 11.00am to 4.00pm.
Steam Working: Every Sunday from Easter until the end of October and certain other dates – please contact the railway for further details.
Prices: Adult £7.00   Child £5.00
                Concessions £6.00
                Family £20.00
Prices are different for special events and are lower than shown above for diesel running days.

Detailed Directions by Car:
From the M4: Exit the M4 at Junction 15 and follow the A419. Turn left towards Blunsdon Stadium and follow the signs for the Railway: From Cirencester: Follow the A419 to the top of Blunsdon Hill, then turn right and follow signs for Blundson Stadium.

TANAT VALLEY LIGHT RAILWAY

Address: Nant Mawr Visitor Centre, Nant Mayr Quarry, Lower Bowl, Nant Mawr, Oswestry   SY10 9HW
Telephone Nº: (01948) 781079
Year Formed: 2004
Location of Line: Nant Mawr Quarry
Length of Line: One third of a mile

Nº of Steam Locos: None
Nº of Other Locos: 3
Nº of Members: 100+
Annual Membership Fee: £10.00
Approx Nº of Visitors P.A.: 5,000+
Gauge: Standard
Web site: www.tvlr.co.uk

GENERAL INFORMATION

Nearest Mainline Station: Gobowen (5 miles)
Nearest Bus Station: Oswestry (5 miles)
Car Parking: Available on site
Coach Parking: None
Souvenir Shop(s): Yes
Food & Drinks: None

SPECIAL INFORMATION

Other attractions at the railway include Woodland Walks, a picnic area and a Nature Trail.

OPERATING INFORMATION

Opening Times: Most weekends from 10.00am to 4.00pm and at other times by prior arrangement. Diesel services operate every weekend throughout August and on National heritage Open Days in September and some other times. Please contact the railway for further information.
Steam Working: None at present.
Prices: No charge although donations are gratefully received.

Detailed Directions by Car:
From All Parts: Take the A5 to the Oswestry bypass then follow the A483 signposted for Welshpool. At the Llynclys Crossroads, turn right onto the A495 and, after about 2 miles, turn right at Blodwell Bank then take the first left and an immediate right turn for the railway.

TANFIELD RAILWAY

Address: Marley Hill Engine Shed, Old Marley Hill, Gateshead, Tyne & Wear NE16 5ET	**Nº of Steam Locos**: 29 Standard, 2 Narrow
	Nº Other Locos: 12 Standard, 15 Narrow
	Nº of Members: 150
Telephone Nº: 0845 463-4938	**Annual Membership Fee**: £10.00 (Adult)
Year Formed: 1976	**Approx Nº of Visitors P.A.**: 40,000
Location of Line: Between Sunniside & East Tanfield, Co. Durham	**Gauge**: Standard and Narrow gauge
	Web site: www.tanfield-railway.co.uk
Length of Line: 3 miles	

GENERAL INFORMATION

Nearest Mainline Station: Newcastle-upon-Tyne (8 miles)
Nearest Bus St'n: Gateshead Interchange (6 miles)
Car Parking: Spaces for 150 cars at Andrews House and 100 spaces at East Tanfield
Coach Parking: Spaces for 6 or 7 coaches only
Souvenir Shop(s): Yes
Food & Drinks: Yes – light snacks only

SPECIAL INFORMATION

Tanfield Railway is the oldest existing railway in use – it was originally opened in 1725. It also runs beside The Causey Arch, the oldest railway bridge in the world.

OPERATING INFORMATION

Opening Times: Every Sunday & Bank Holiday Monday throughout the year. Also opens on Wednesdays & Thursdays in Summer school holidays. Santa Specials run in December.
Steam Working: Most trains are steam-hauled and run from 11.00am to 4.00pm (11.30am to 3.30pm in the Winter). Trains on Thursdays are diesel-hauled.
Prices: Adult £9.00
      Child £5.00 (Under 5's travel free)
      Senior Citizen £6.00
      Family £23.00 (2 adults + 2 children)
Note: Higher prices may be charged on Special Event days.

Detailed Directions by Car:
Sunniside Station is off the A6076 Sunniside to Stanley road in Co. Durham. To reach the Railway, leave A1(M), follow signs for Beamish museum at Chester-le-Street then continue to Stanley and follow Tanfield Railway signs.

TELFORD STEAM RAILWAY

Address: The Old Loco Shed, Bridge Road, Horsehay, Telford, Shropshire
Telephone Enquiries: 07876 762790
Year Formed: 1976
Location: Horsehay & Dawley Station
Length of Line: ½ mile standard gauge, an eighth of a mile 2 foot narrow gauge

N° of Steam Locos: 5 (not operational)
N° of Other Locos: 12
N° of Members: Approximately 220
Annual Membership Fee: £12.00
Approx N° of Visitors P.A.: 10,000
Web site: www.telfordsteamrailway.co.uk

GENERAL INFORMATION

Nearest Mainline Station: Wellington or Telford Central
Nearest Bus Station: Dawley (1 mile)
Car Parking: Free parking at the site
Coach Parking: Free parking at the site
Souvenir Shop(s): 'Freight Stop Gift Shop'
Food & Drinks: 'The Furnaces' Tea Room

SPECIAL INFORMATION

Telford Steam Railway has both a Standard Gauge and Narrow Gauge line as well as Miniature and Model Railways. Major line extension works are currently underway.

OPERATING INFORMATION

Opening Times: Every Sunday and Bank Holiday between Easter and the end of September. Santa Specials run in December. Open 11.00am to 4.30pm.
Steam Working: Only the 2 foot gauge is currently in steam on operating days as the Standard gauge engine is undergoing repairs.
Prices: Adult all day tickets £5.00
Child all day tickets £3.00
Family all day tickets £12.00
Note: Higher prices apply for special event days.

Detailed Directions by Car:
From All Parts: Exit the M54 at Junction 6, travel south along the A5223 then follow the brown tourist signs for the railway.

THE WEARDALE RAILWAY

Address: Stanhope Station, Stanhope, Bishop Auckland DL13 2YS	**N° of Steam Locos:** 1
Telephone N°: (01388) 526203	**N° of Other Locos:** 4 (including DMUs)
Year Formed: 1993	**N° of Members:** 850
Location: Stanhope to Bishop Auckland, County Durham	**Approx N° of Visitors P.A.:** 25,000
	Gauge: Standard
Length of Line: 16 miles at present	**Web site:** www.weardale-railway.org.uk

GENERAL INFORMATION

Nearest Mainline Station: Bishop Auckland (¼ mile)
Nearest Bus Station: Bishop Auckland
Car Parking: Available at both Stanhope and Wolsingham Stations
Coach Parking: Available at Wolsingham Station
Souvenir Shop(s): Yes
Food & Drinks: Yes – Signal Box Cafe, Stanhope

SPECIAL INFORMATION

Weardale is in the heart of the North Pennines and the railway provides magnificent unspoilt views. The area is known for its footpaths and bridleways and the railway provides a useful base for walks between stations along banks of the beautiful River Wear.

OPERATING INFORMATION

Opening Times: See below
Steam Working: See below

NOTE: At the time of going to press, the American owners of the railway had suspended all passenger services pending further notice. However, it is expected that number services will run later in 2013. Please contact the railway for further information about the dates and nature of these services.

Detailed Directions by Car:

From All Parts: Stanhope Station is located in Stanhope, just off the A689; Bishop Auckland West Station is a short walk from the Northern Rail Mainline Station in Bishop Auckland (SatNavs use DL14 7TL).

WENSLEYDALE RAILWAY

Address: Leeming Bar Station, Leases Road, Leeming Bar, Northallerton DL7 9AR	**Nº of Steam Locos**: Visiting locos only
Telephone Nº: 08454 50 54 74	**Nº of Other Locos**: Various Diesel locos
Year Formed: The railway association was formed in 1990, the Railway PLC in 2000.	**Nº of Members**: 3,500
Location of Line: Leeming Bar to Redmire	**Annual Membership Fee**: £15.00
Length of Line: Approximately 16 miles	**Approx Nº of Visitors P.A.**: Not known
	Gauge: Standard
	Web site: www.wensleydalerail.com

GENERAL INFORMATION

Nearest Mainline Station: Northallerton (7 miles)
Nearest Bus Station: Northallerton (7 miles)
Car & Coach Parking: Available at Leeming Bar, Leyburn and Redmire Stations
Souvenir Shop(s): Yes
Food & Drinks: At Leeming Bar & Leyburn stations.

SPECIAL INFORMATION

Most services are operated via DMU and travel to Leyburn & Redmire tourist destinations in the Wensleydale Valley. Other heritage diesel groups also use the line.

OPERATING INFORMATION

Opening Times: Weekends only during off-peak time. Open daily during school holidays and most days (except Wednesdays & Thursdays) from 28th March to 3rd November. Also other selected dates in November, Santa Specials in December and on New Year's Day. Contact the railway for further details.
Steam Working: Visiting steam locos will operate on some dates from 25th April to 28th November 2013. Please contact the railway for further information.
Prices: Adult Return £12.50   Child Return £6.25
Senior Citizen Return £11.00
Family Day Rover £22.50 – £30.00
Note: Single and return tickets cost less depending on destination. Prices may differ during steam working.

Detailed Directions by Car:
From All Parts: Exit the A1 at the Leeming Bar exit and take the A684 towards Northallerton. The station is on the left after about ¼ mile close to the road junction and after the traffic lights.   By Bus: The Dales & District 73 bus route travels between Northallerton and Leeming Bar.

WEST SOMERSET RAILWAY

Address: The Railway Station, Minehead, Somerset TA24 5BG	**Nº of Steam Locos**: 7
Telephone Nº: (01643) 704996 (enquiries)	**Nº of Other Locos**: 12
Year Formed: 1976	**Nº of Members**: 5,000
Location of Line: Bishops Lydeard (near Taunton) to Minehead	**Annual Membership Fee**: £19.00
	Approx Nº of Visitors P.A.: 210,000
Length of Line: 19¾ miles	**Gauge**: Standard
	Web site: www.west-somerset-railway.co.uk

Photo courtesy of Sam Burton/West Somerset Railway

GENERAL INFORMATION

Nearest Mainline Station: Taunton (4 miles)
Nearest Bus Station: Taunton (4½ miles) – Service 28s run to Bishops Lydeard.
Car Parking: Free parking at Bishops Lydeard; Council car parking at Minehead and Watchet
Coach Parking: As above
Souvenir Shop(s): Yes – at Minehead, Bishops Lydeard and Washford
Food & Drinks: Yes – At some stations. Buffet cars on most trains.

SPECIAL INFORMATION

Britain's longest Standard gauge Heritage railway runs through the Quantock Hills and along the Bristol Channel Coast. The line passes through no fewer than ten Stations with museums at Washford and Blue Anchor and a turntable at Minehead.

OPERATING INFORMATION

Opening Times: 2013 dates: Various dates from February to December including daily from 18th May to 6th October. Open 9.30am to 5.30pm. Please contact the railway for more detailed dates.
Steam Working: All operating days except during Diesel Galas.
Prices: Adult Day Rover £17.00
              Child Day Rover £8.50
              Family Rover £45.00 (2 adult + 4 child)
              Senior Citizen Day Rover £15.40

Detailed Directions by Car:
Exit the M5 at Taunton (Junction 25) and follow signs for A358 to Williton and then the A39 for Minehead. In Minehead, brown tourist signs give directions to the railway.

WHITWELL & REEPHAM RAILWAY

Address: Whitwell Road, Reepham, Norfolk NR10 4GA
Telephone Nº: (01603) 871694
Year Formed: 2009
Location of Line: Norfolk
Length of Line: Almost ½ mile

Nº of Steam Locos: 1
Nº of Other Locos: 1
Nº of Members: Approximately 400
Annual Membership Fee: £15.00
Approx Nº of Visitors P.A.: 6,000
Gauge: Standard
Web site: www.whitwellstation.com

GENERAL INFORMATION

Nearest Mainline Station: Norwich (15 miles)
Nearest Bus Station: Norwich (15 miles)
Car Parking: Available on site
Coach Parking: Available
Souvenir Shop(s): Yes
Food & Drinks: Available

SPECIAL INFORMATION

Whitwell & Reepham Station re-opened on the 28th February 2009 nearly 50 years after it was closed to passengers on 2nd March 1959. The intention is to restore the Station to its former glory, re-laying of track and sidings, acquiring rolling stock and setting up a museum relating to the Station and The Midland & Great Northern Railway.

OPERATING INFORMATION

Opening Times: Weekends throughout the year from 10.00am until 5.00pm.
Steam Working: 2013 dates: 20th & 21st April; 2nd & 16th June; 6th, 7th, 27th & 28th July; 25th August; 27th & 29th September. Santa Specials run on 7th, 8th, 13th, 15th, 20th & 22nd December.
Prices: Adults £2.00
Children £1.00
Family £5.00
Note: Prices shown above are for train rides – admission to the museum is free of charge.

Detailed Directions by Car:
From All Parts: Take the A1067 Norwich to Fakenham Road to Bawdeswell then follow the B1145 to Reepham. The railway is located about 1 mile to the South-west of Reepham and is well-signposted.

YEOVIL RAILWAY CENTRE

Address: Yeovil Junction Station, Stoford, Yeovil BA22 9UU **Telephone Nº**: (01935) 410420 **Year Formed**: 1994 **Location of Line**: Yeovil Junction **Length of Line**: ¼ mile **Gauge**: Standard	**Nº of Steam Locos**: 1 (2 from mid-2013) **Nº of Other Locos**: 4 **Nº of Members**: 300 **Annual Membership Fee**: £15.00 **Approx Nº of Visitors P.A.**: 5,000 **Web site**: www.yeovilrailway.freeservers.com

GENERAL INFORMATION

Nearest Mainline Station: Yeovil Junction (adjacent)
Nearest Bus Station: A regular bus service runs Monday to Saturday from Yeovil Bus Station (2 miles)
Car Parking: Available on site
Coach Parking: Available nearby
Souvenir Shop(s): Yes
Food & Drinks: Available

SPECIAL INFORMATION

The Visitor Centre is located in a GWR Transfer Shed which was built in 1864.
The centre also runs Driver Experience days.

OPERATING INFORMATION

Opening Times: Open regularly for Steam Train days, Mainline steam visits and other special events from March to October. Also open for Santa Specials in December and for static viewing every Sunday morning from 10.00am until noon. Please contact the Centre for further details of event days.
Steam Working: Numerous operating days throughout the summer. Please contact the Centre for further details.
Prices: Adult £6.00
　　　　　Child £3.00 (Ages 5 to 15)
One child is admitted free with each paying adult
Note: Prices shown above are for Steam Working days.

Detailed Directions by Car:
The Centre is part of Yeovil Junction Station which is served by South West Trains. By road simply follow the signs to Yeovil Junction Station from Yeovil town centre or from the A37 Dorchester to Yeovil road. The entrance to Yeovil Railway Centre is through the low bridge, half way up the Yeovil Junction Station approach road.